The GUITARIS to Sight Reading

by Jerry Jennings

INTRO

The goal of this book is to take the non-reading guitarist, step by step, into the world of reading. As you progress through *The Guitarist's Link to Sight Reading*, you will find tunes that have been written specifically to work with the exercises. Once you've played through the song a time or two, try it with the CD. The tracks are of a live band, without the melody. I've also included versions *with* the melody at the end of the CD. Until you are solid on any given tune, refrain from listening to the melody version. The first time you hear these melodies, I want them to come from your guitar. Thanks, and enjoy!

FOR GUITARISTS WHO DESIRE TO READ MUSIC AND FOLLOW CHARTS

Cover photograph—Thomas Bass
Interior design and layout—Jane Jennings

Jerry Jennings—Guitar / Erik Kleven—Bass
Dave Blank—Drums (except Funky Weather by Greg Dana) Jeff Tuttle—Percussion

This book Copyright © 1994 by Jerry Jennings

All rights reserved. No part of this book may be reproduced in any form or by any electronic or mechanical means, including information storage and retrieval systems, without permission in writing from the publisher.

Order No. JJ 10000
International Standard Book Number: 0-9700038-0-3

Exclusive Distributors:
Music Sales Corporation 257 Park Avenue South, New York, NY 10010 USA
Music Sales Limited 8/9 Frith Street, London W1D 3JB England
Music Sales Pty. Limited 120 Rothschild Street, Rosebery, Sydney, NSW 2018, Australia

Printed in the United States of America by Vicks Lithograph & Printing Corporation

Visit **J. Jennings Publishing Company** on the internet at http://www.jenningspub.com

J. JENNINGS PUBLISHING COMPANY

CONTENTS

BASICS		4
LESSON 1	Lower Triad A, C, & E	6
	Note Values	6
	Exercise 1	7
LESSON 2	Higher Triad E, A, & C	8
	Rolling Technique	8
	Exercise 2	9
LESSON 3	Lower Group B & D	10
	Exercise 3	11
LESSON 4	Higher Group G & B	12
	Quarter Rest	12
	Exercise 4	13
SONG EXERCISE #1	Repeat Sign	14
	Rhythm Pattern	14
	Half Rest	14
	"Avocados"	15
SONG EXERCISE #2	1st and 2nd Endings	16
	"Traces of Thought"	17
SONG EXERCISE #3	New Time Signature $\frac{3}{4}$	18
	Rhythm Pattern	18
	Traffic Signs: D.C. al Coda / Double Lines / Rehearsal Letters	18
	"Mirrors on Pluto"	19
PENCILQUIZ 1		20
LESSON 5	Middle G & A	22
	Ties	22
	Exercise 5	23
LESSON 6	Middle C & D	24
	Whole Rest	24
	Exercise 6	25
PENTATONIC THRILLS #1		26
	A Minor or C Major Pentatonic Scale	26
	Pentatonic Thrill #1	27
PENCILQUIZ 2		28
LESSON 7	Add Lower F	30
	Eighth Notes	30
	Exercise 7	31
LESSON 8	Add Higher F	32
	Exercise 8	33

SONG EXERCISE #4	Staccato	34
	Whole Rests in $\frac{3}{4}$ Time	34
	"Rebel Without a Pause"	35
SONG EXERCISE #5	Power Chords / Rhythm Pattern	36
	"Bar None"	37
LESSON 9	Middle B	38
	Dotted Quarter Note	38
	Grace Note	39
	Exercise 9	39
PENTATONIC THRILLS #2		40
	Pull Offs (p/o)	40
	Pentatonic Thrill #2	41
LESSON 10	Flats	42
	Natural Sign	42
	Eighth Rest	42
	Exercise 10	43
LESSON 11	Sharps	44
	Natural Sign	44
	Exercise 11	45
PENTATONIC THRILLS #3		46
	C Minor / D Minor / G Minor / E Minor Pentatonic Scales	46
	Pentatonic Thrill #3	47
LESSON 12	New Time Signatures $\frac{6}{8}$ & $\frac{12}{8}$	48
	Dotted Quarter Rest	48
	Dotted Whole Note	48
	Exercise 12	49
SONG EXERCISE #6	Key Signature (key of G)	50
	Traffic Signs: D.S. / Repeat Loop	50
	Slash Chords	50
	"Funky Weather"	51
SONG EXERCISE #7	Shuffle / Pick Up Notes / More on Keys	52
	"Some Kinda Blues"	53
SONG EXERCISE #8	Another Key Signature (Key of F)	54
	Traffic Sign: Al Fine	54
	Dotted Half Note	54
	"Bossa de Hot Sauce"	55
CD CONTENTS		56
APPENDIX #1	Chords	57
APPENDIX #2	Key Signatures	62

BASICS

THE STAFF *Consists of five lines and four spaces.*

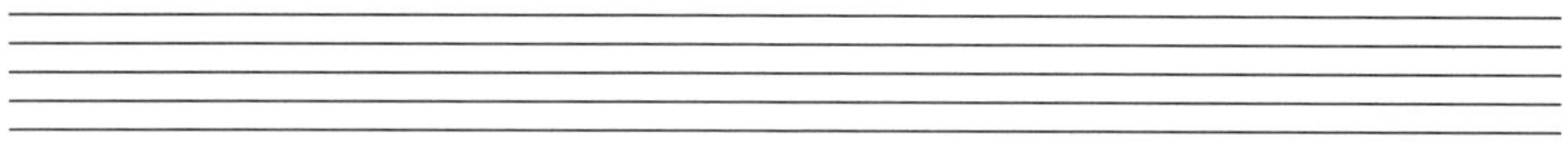

THE TREBLE CLEF *Circles the "G" line and is sometimes called the G clef.*

TIME SIGNATURE

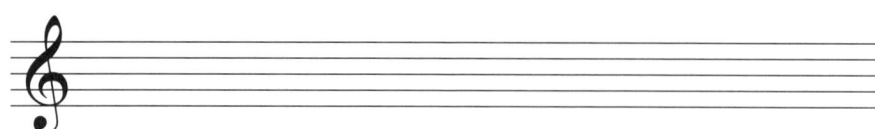

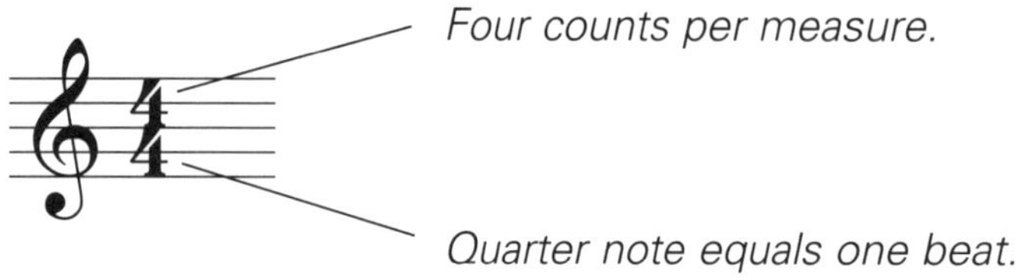

— *Four counts per measure.*

— *Quarter note equals one beat.*

KEY SIGNATURE *This example shows the key of D (See Appendix 2).*

MEASURES & BARLINES

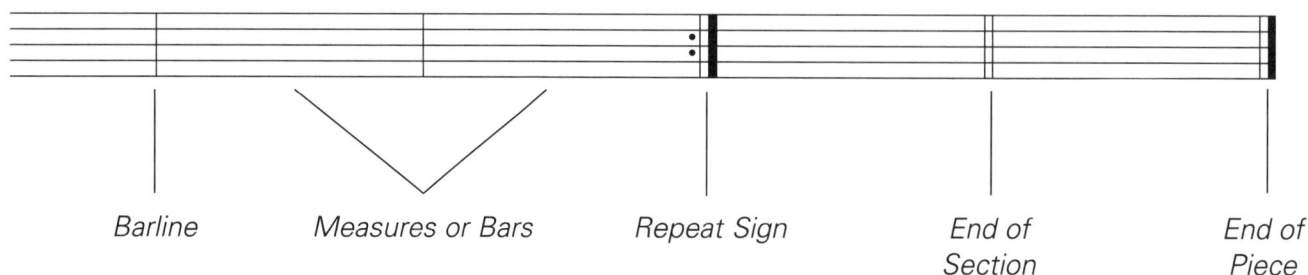

Barline   Measures or Bars   Repeat Sign   End of Section   End of Piece

NAMES OF LINES AND SPACES *For the treble clef.*

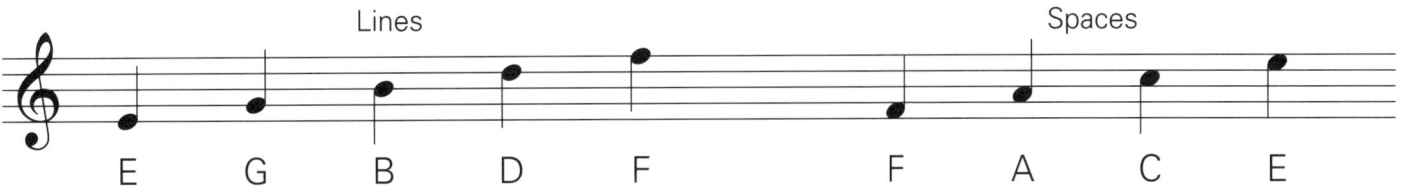

LEGER LINES *When notes are higher or lower than the staff, leger lines are used.*

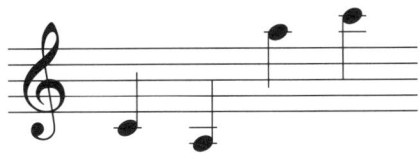

TIME VALUES OF NOTES AND RESTS

Whole Note / Whole Rest

Half Notes / Half Rests

Quarter Notes / Quarter Rests

Eighth Notes / Eighth Rests

Sixteenth Notes / Sixteenth Rests

Lesson 1

Lower Triad A, C, & E

The first three notes we'll be using are a low **A**, **C**, and **E**. At this time it will be very beneficial to assign one finger to each fret.

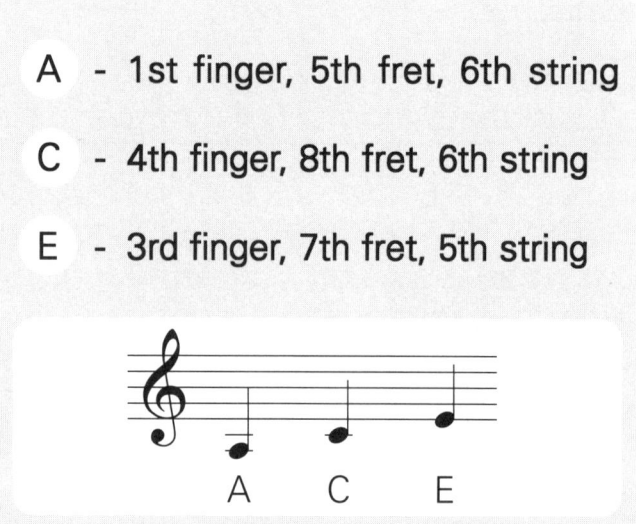

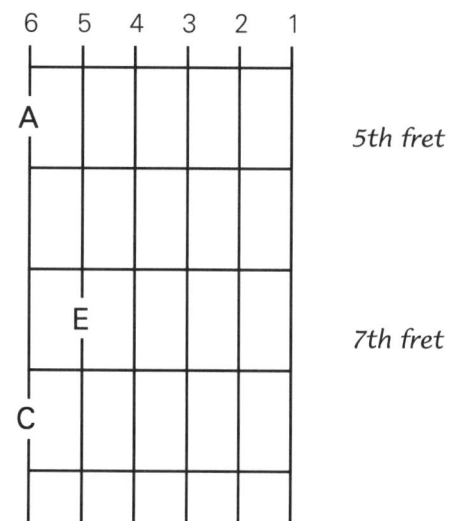

5th fret

7th fret

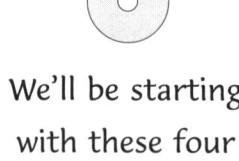
Tracks 1-4

We'll be starting with these four note values.

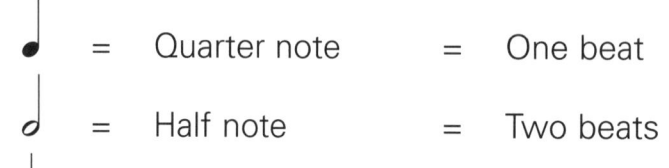

♩ = Quarter note = One beat

𝅗𝅥 = Half note = Two beats

𝅗𝅥. = Dotted half note = Three beats *(a dot after any note means increase its value by half)*

𝅝 = Whole note = Four beats

$\frac{4}{4}$ time, also known as common time (**C**)

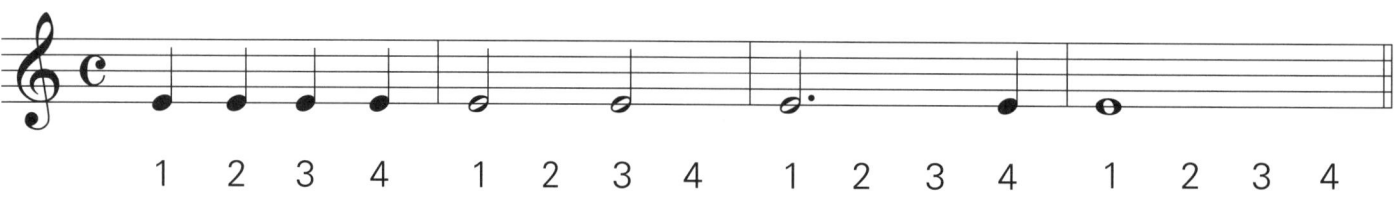

| 1 2 3 4 | 1 2 3 4 | 1 2 3 4 | 1 2 3 4 |

Keep a steady beat, either by tapping your foot or with a metronome. Included on the CD are four metronome tracks, ranging from slow to fast. The slowest (track 5) is 70 bpm, and the fastest (track 8) is 130 bpm. Use the slowest at first and pick up the tempo as you become more proficient.

Try playing up and down the notes a few times:

A C E C

First go through Exercise 1 using just <u>one</u> note (pretend they're all A notes), nailing the time values only. Pick all down strokes. Keep your eyes on the page.

Tracks 5-8

EXERCISE 1

It's important to keep the left-hand fingers parallel to the frets, thumb vertical and low, so your wrist is free of the neck.

When playing through the exercise, resist the temptation to leave fingers 1 and 3 in place. This would cause more than one note to ring at a time. Also, your fingers need to get used to finding the notes.

7

Lesson 2

Higher Triad E, A, & C

Now we'll be working with the higher notes of the 5th position—**E**, **A**, and **C**.

- **E** - 1st finger, 5th fret, 2nd string
- **A** - 1st finger, 5th fret, 1st string
- **C** - 4th finger, 8th fret, 1st string

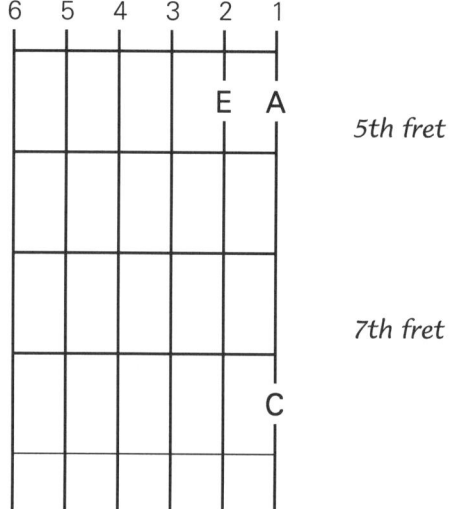

The general rule is to use your fingertips, but when two notes on adjacent strings are on the same fret, like the *E* and *A* shown above, sometimes it's better to use a roll. Make sure to deaden each note as you play the next one. You should hear only one note at a time. Example: When playing the *E* note, you're on the fingertip—now collapse it to play the *A*. Make sure to collapse it far enough to deaden the *E*.

ROLLING: The primary motion is the collapsing and rebounding of the outermost knuckle (the one closest to the nail) on your left hand.

8

Let's try playing up and down the new notes:

E   A   C   A

. . . .

Again, don't leave your fingers on unused notes. Keep your eyes on the page.

Tracks 5-8

EXERCISE 2

. . . .

Work on Exercises 1 & 2 for a good week before plunging ahead. Even if this seems simple, it can get quite confusing if you start piling on more notes too soon.

9

Lesson 3
Lower Group B & D

Let's add **B** and **D** to the lower group.

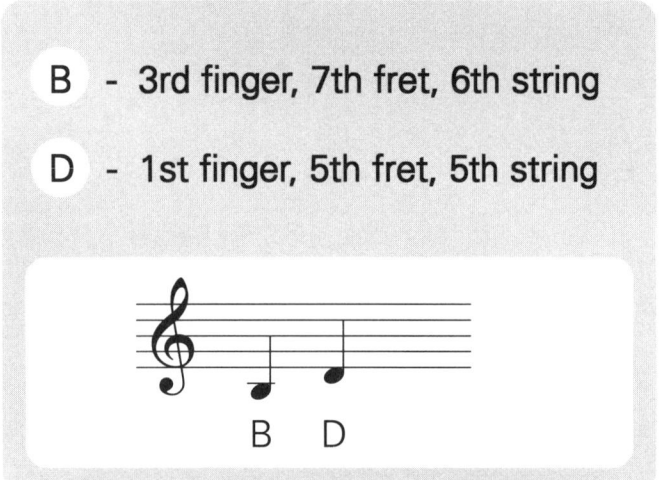

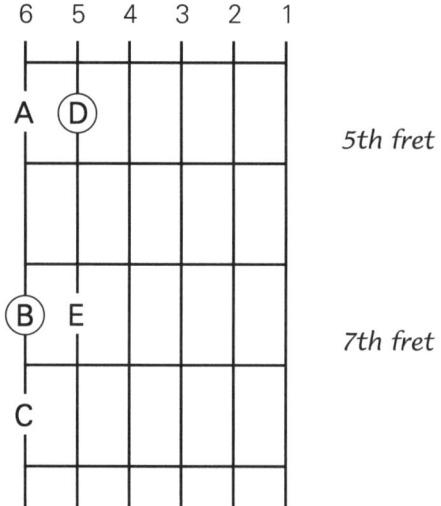

5th fret

7th fret

There will be more rolling action possible now, because the **A** and **D** share the same fret, and so do **B** and **E**. When rolling from **D to A,** or **E to B,** try to end up on your fingertip.

Play up and down all five notes of the lower group. Get used to the notes and remember, one finger per fret. This can also serve as a note reference.

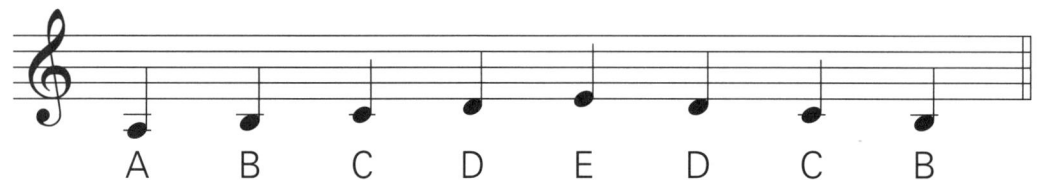

10

EXERCISE 3

Tracks 5-8

Maintain a steady count and keep your eyes on the page.

Lesson 4
Higher Group G & B

Here are two more notes in the higher group, **G** and **B**. Notice we've started with the outside strings, and we're working our way in toward the middle of the fretboard.

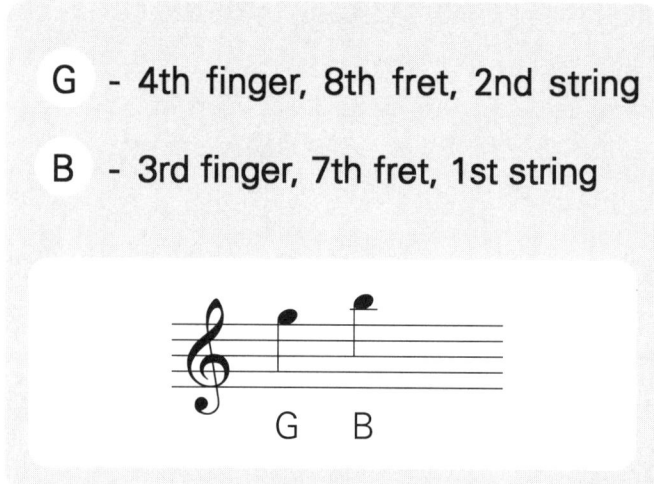

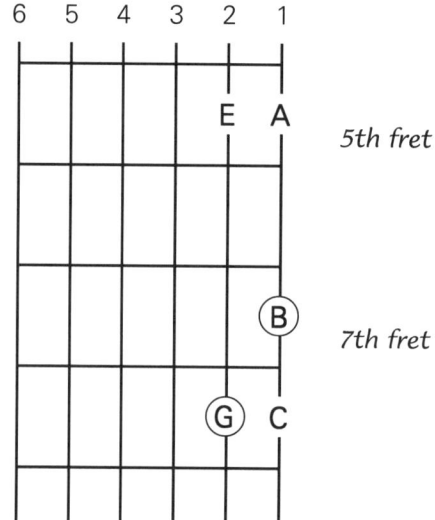

A rest is a note of silence. It can be achieved by easing up your left-hand finger from the string that's ringing. Don't lift your finger all the way off the string, just enough to stop the ring. Be sure to use good timing on rests, as you do with notes. They can be very effective when timed properly.

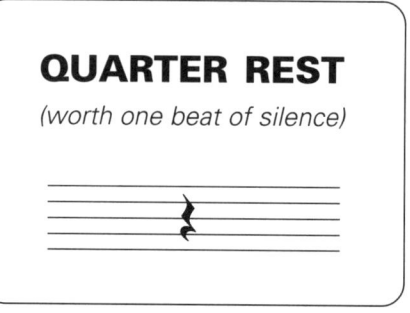

QUARTER REST
(worth one beat of silence)

Note Reference

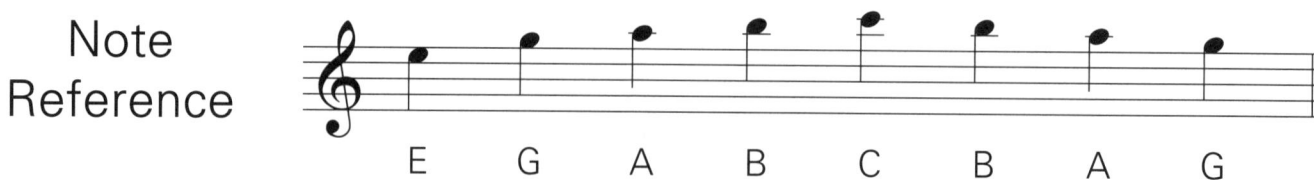

E G A B C B A G

FOOD FOR THOUGHT | When playing, rather than concentrating on the length of the note presently ringing, focus on when the next note should arrive. If you hit the note at the right time, the preceding note will automatically be the right length.

Tracks 5-8

EXERCISE 4

SONG EXERCISE #1: *Avocados*

Notice the repeat sign at the end of bar four. When you reach this sign, go back to the beginning and repeat the first four bars (also known as measures), then continue on to the end of the song.

The end of a song is indicated by this type of bar line. Notice it's a double line (one thin line and one thick). It is similar to the repeat sign, but has no dots.

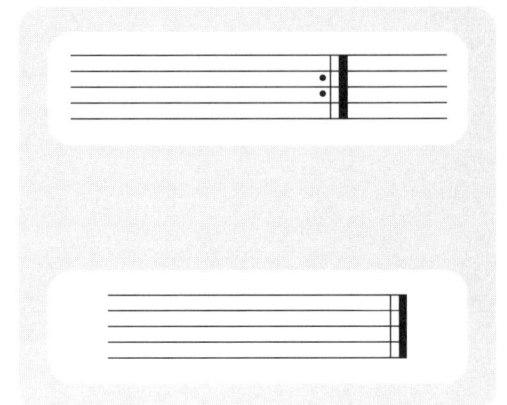

The chords written above the staff can be played by someone else while you play the melody, or you play the chords while someone else plays the melody. For starters, use this rhythm, accenting on beat 1 and 3 of each measure. In the last measure, just strum once and let it ring.

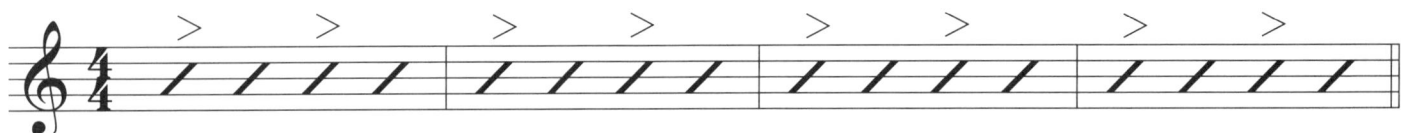

HALF REST
(worth two beats of silence)

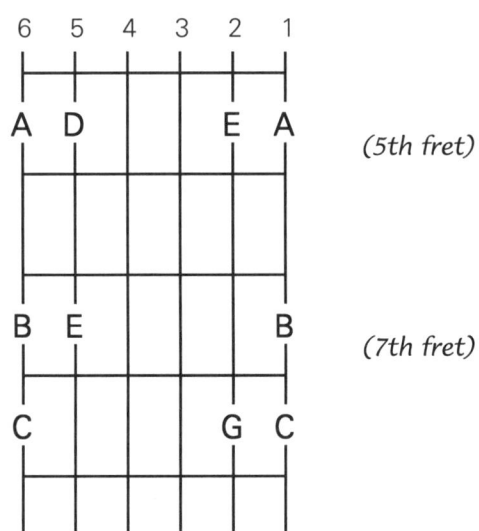

Note Reference

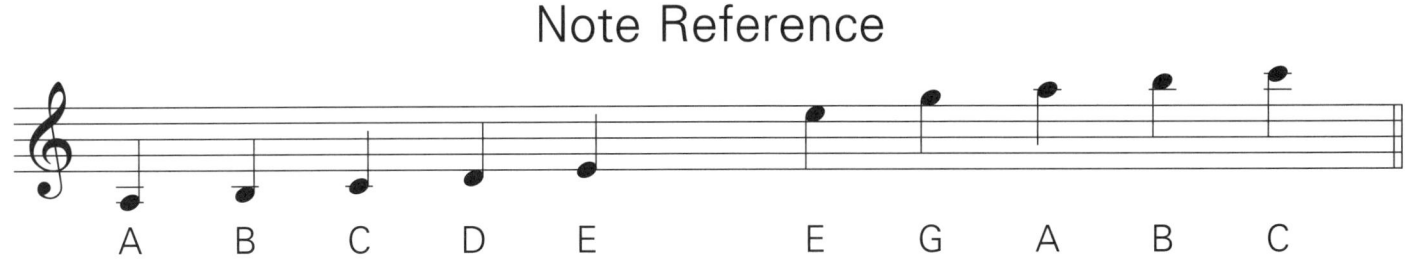

Avocados

Jerry Jennings

SONG EXERCISE #2: *Traces of Thought*

1st and 2nd Endings

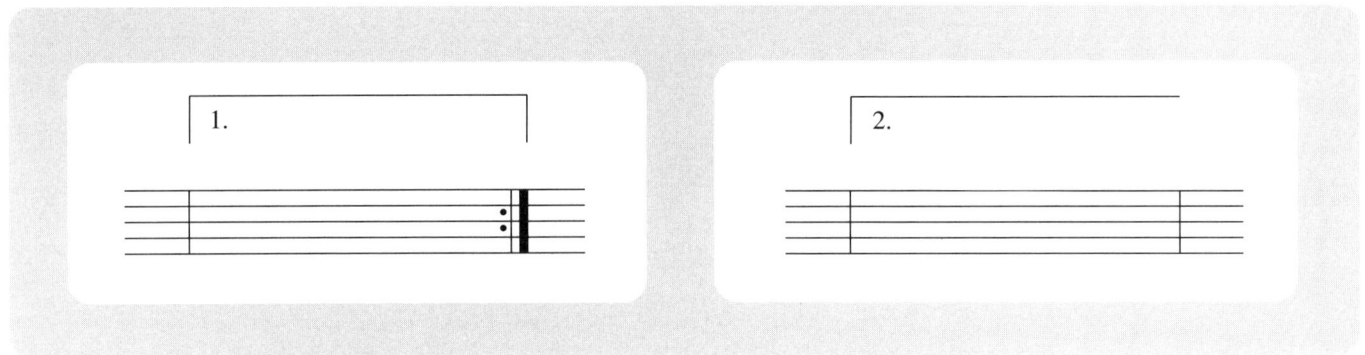

Play to the end of bar four (1st ending, repeat sign). Now go back to the beginning and continue the song, this time skipping bar four and going straight to bar five (2nd ending). By doing this, the first line will be a total of eight bars.

Make sure you play through the song rhythmically first (on just one note).

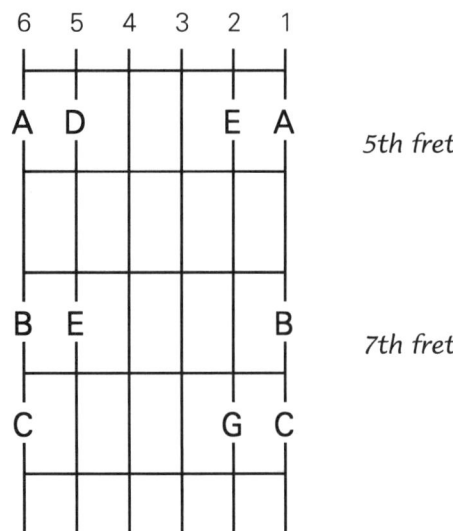

Note Reference

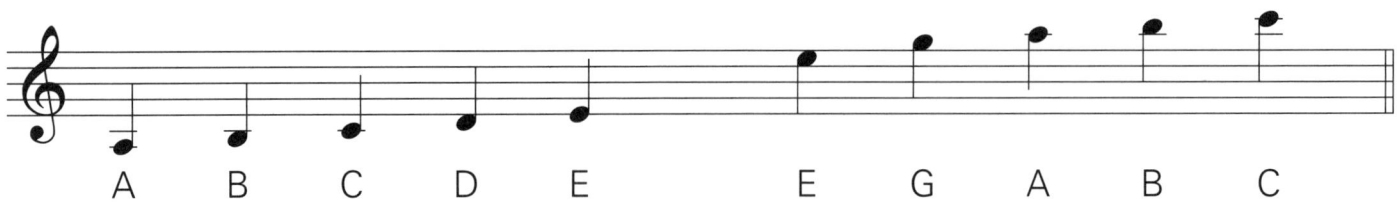

Traces of Thought

Jerry Jennings

Track 10

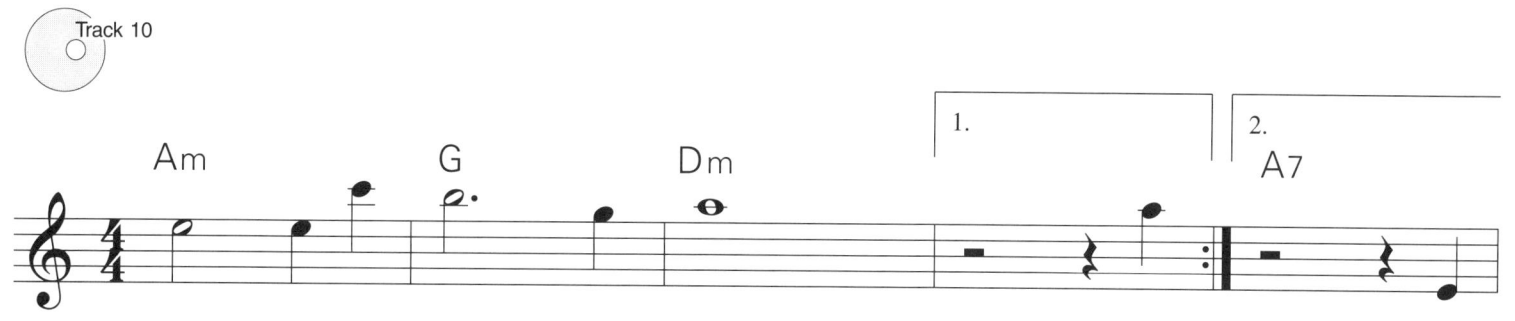
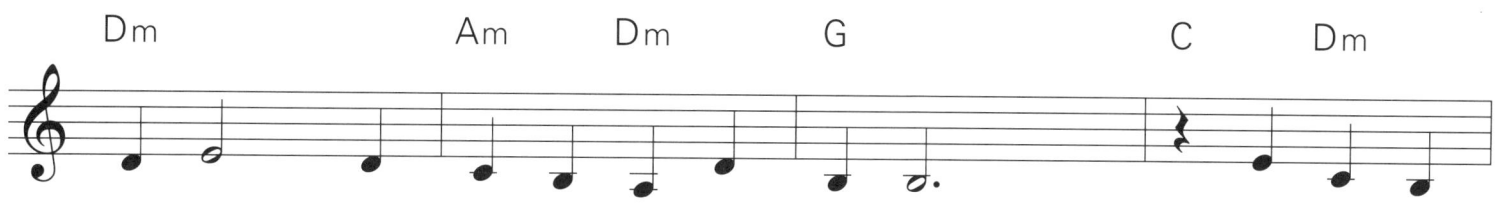

SONG EXERCISE #3: *Mirrors on Pluto*

3/4 Introducing a new time signature: 3/4. In this song, we'll be playing three beats per measure. A common mistake when first learning 3/4 timing is to pause after the third count (Example: 123_123_). This is actually 4/4 time because the extra beat is functional, whether silent or not. Make sure that when you *would* be saying four, you're saying one and counting on from there (Example: 123123123).

Rhythm players accent on beat 1 of each measure.

Traffic Signs

D.C. al Coda - This is one of many signs that can be used to fit very long songs neatly on a page or two. ***D.C.*** *(da Capo)* means go back to the beginning of the song. ***al Coda*** means once you've gone back to the beginning (D.C.), you play to the first coda sign (⊕) then skip down to the second coda sign and play from the second coda sign to the end. Got that?

Thin double lines indicate the end of a section.

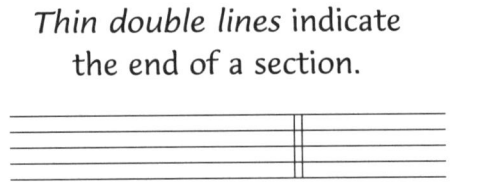

Letters in boxes (A & B & C) can be used to label sections. They're called *rehearsal letters*.

Trace the form of the song visually a time or two before playing through it. This song is thirty-three bars long (don't forget the repeat at the end of bar six). Make sure you play through the song rhythmically first (on just one note).

Note Reference

A B C D E   E G A B C

Mirrors on Pluto

Jerry Jennings

Pencilquiz 1

1. Draw a few quarter notes:

    The stem should be one octave long (3 1/2 spaces or 3 1/2 lines)

    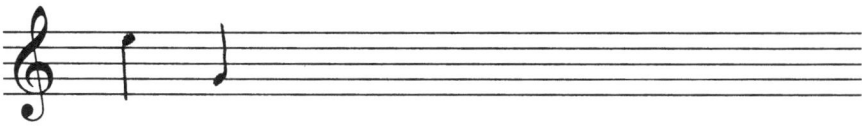

2. Draw a few half notes:

    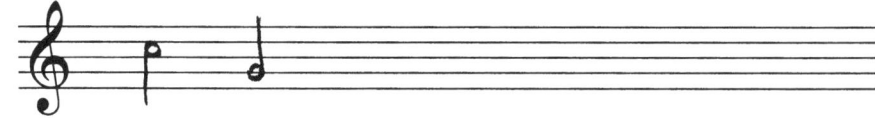

3. Draw a few whole notes:

    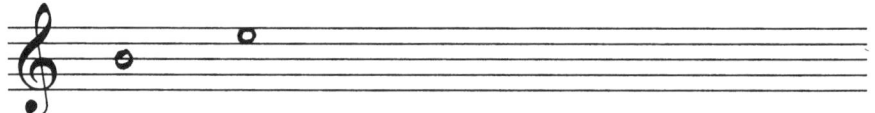

4. Draw a few half rests:

    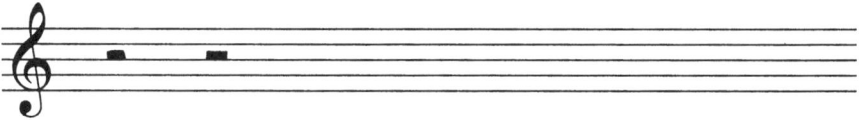

5. Draw a few quarter rests:

    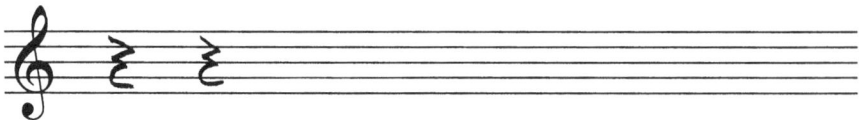

6. Draw some dotted half notes:

    The dot should be on a space, even if the note is on a line.

    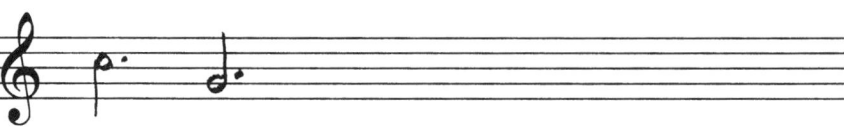

You write this exercise. Be creative if you want to, but mainly what's important is that you can play it. Use the notes and rests you've learned so far. Note spacing within the measure is also important. Just visualize four beats and try to align each note over the beat it gets played (see bar one).

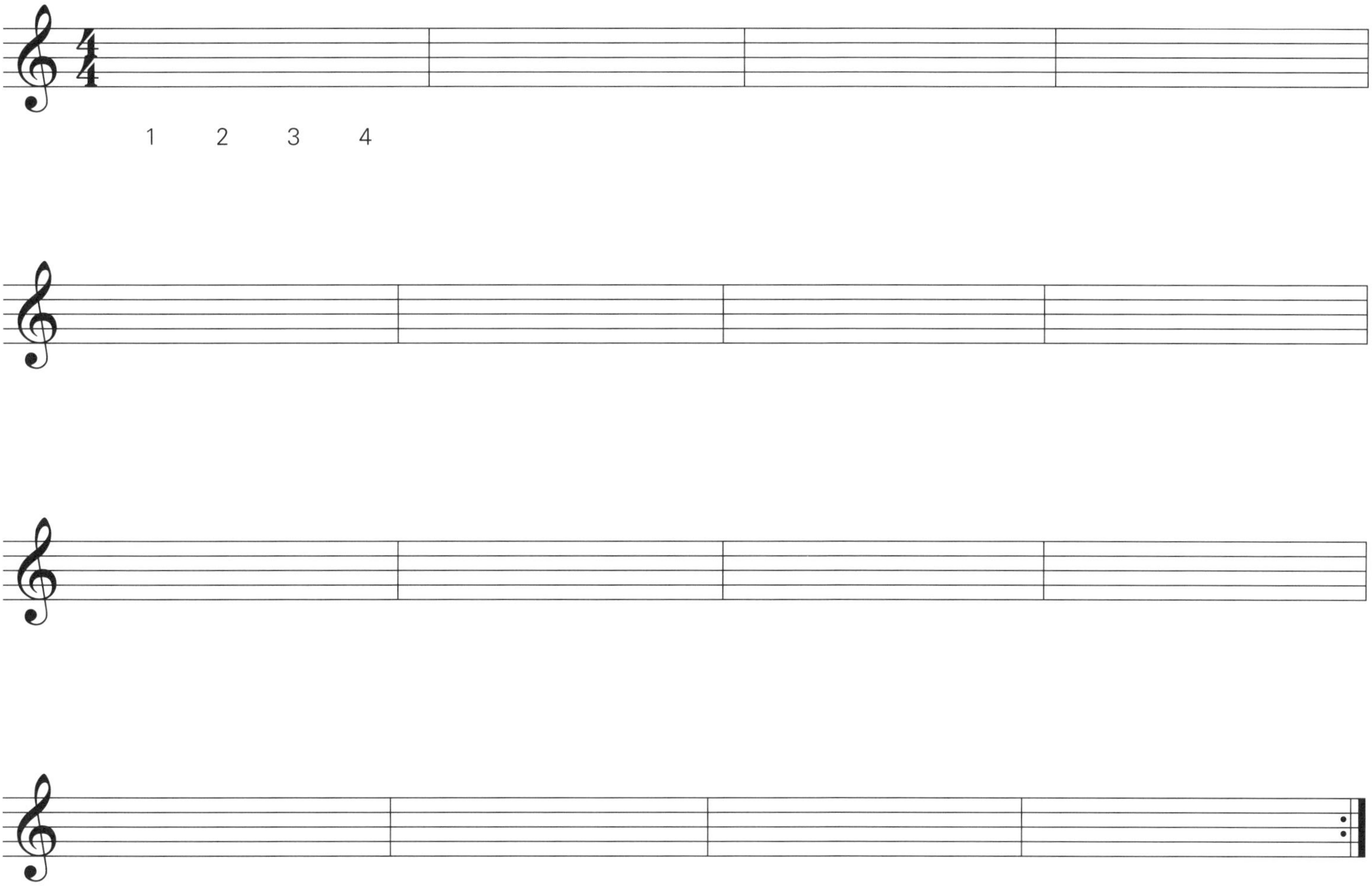

1 2 3 4

Note Reference

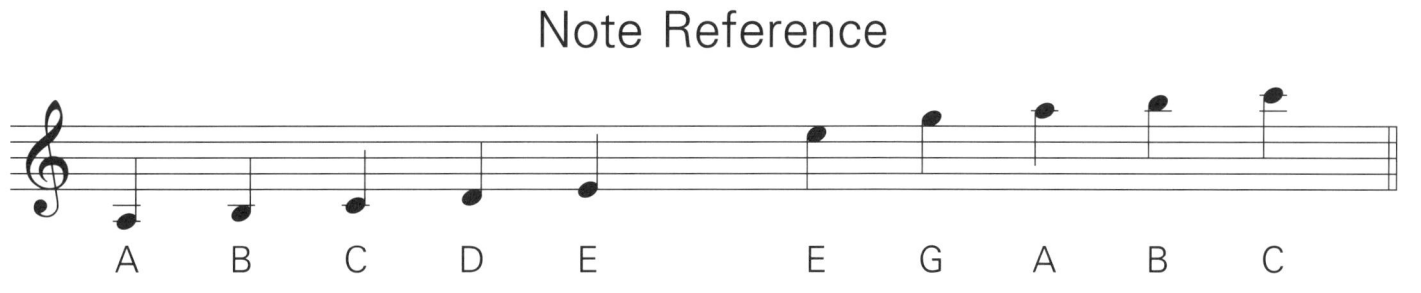

Lesson 5
Middle G & A

We have finally arrived at the middle of the neck for the lower group! Here's the **G** and **A**.

G - 1st finger, 5th fret, 4th string

A - 3rd finger, 7th fret, 4th string

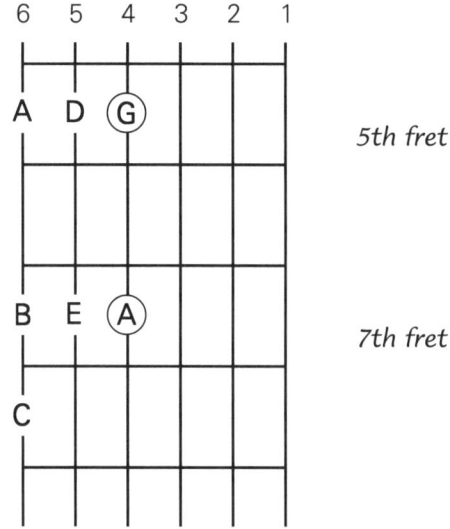

TIES

When two notes are tied together, play the first note and add the value of the note it's tied to. Example: If you see a quarter note tied to another quarter note, that is worth two counts (same as a half note). Notice the first beat of bar two. There is no need to pick that note because it's tied to the fourth note of bar one and will still be ringing.

Note Reference

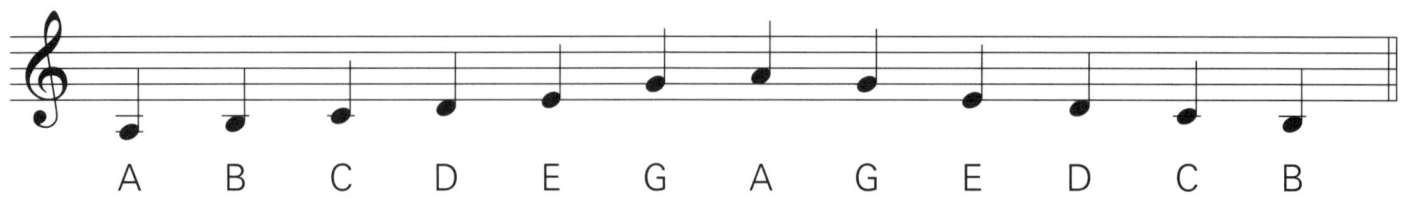

A B C D E G A G E D C B

22

Why use a tie? Here's one example: Say you want to play a half note starting on beat 4. You can only fit one more beat in that measure, so you must "tie" into the following measure to complete the value of the half note.

EXERCISE 5

*K*eep a steady count, planting each note firmly on the beat.

Lesson 6
Middle C & D

The upper group is nearing completion, with the addition of **C** and **D**.

C - 1st finger, 5th fret, 3rd string

D - 3rd finger, 7th fret, 3rd string

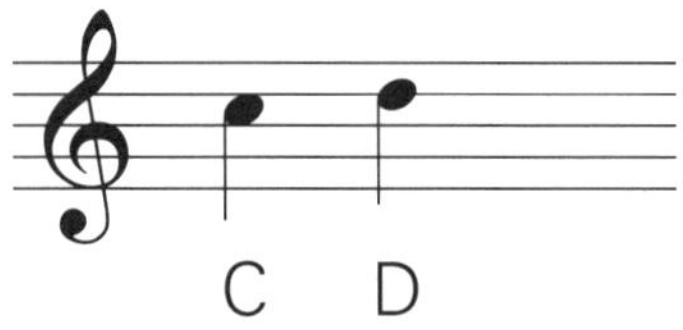

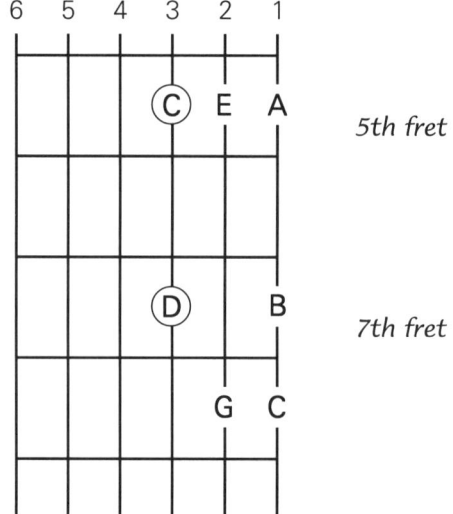

The whole rest is similar to the half rest in appearance, but it hangs from the fourth line instead of sitting on the third. It's worth FOUR beats of silence.

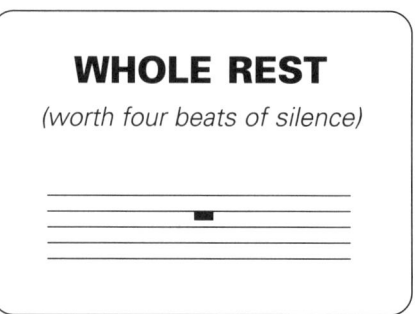

WHOLE REST
(worth four beats of silence)

Note Reference

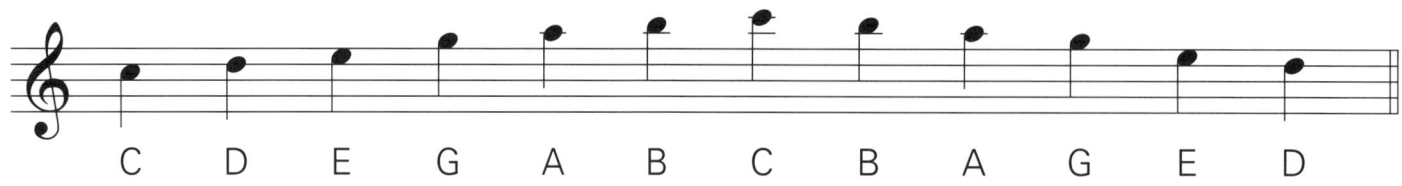

C D E G A B C B A G E D

EXERCISE 6

The lower and higher group have joined. Now it will be possible to indulge in some cheap pentatonic thrills!

Pentatonic Thrills #1

As the name implies, a pentatonic scale has only five notes. In this example, the five notes are **A, C, D, E, G**. It's actually a whittled down version of a seven-note scale.

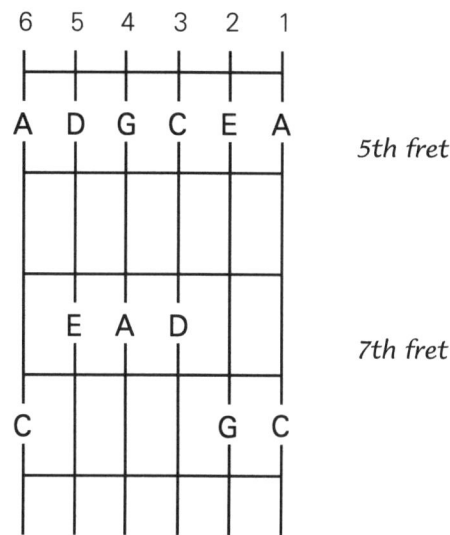

This scale could either be called the *A minor pentatonic* or the *C major pentatonic*, depending on which note is emphasized.

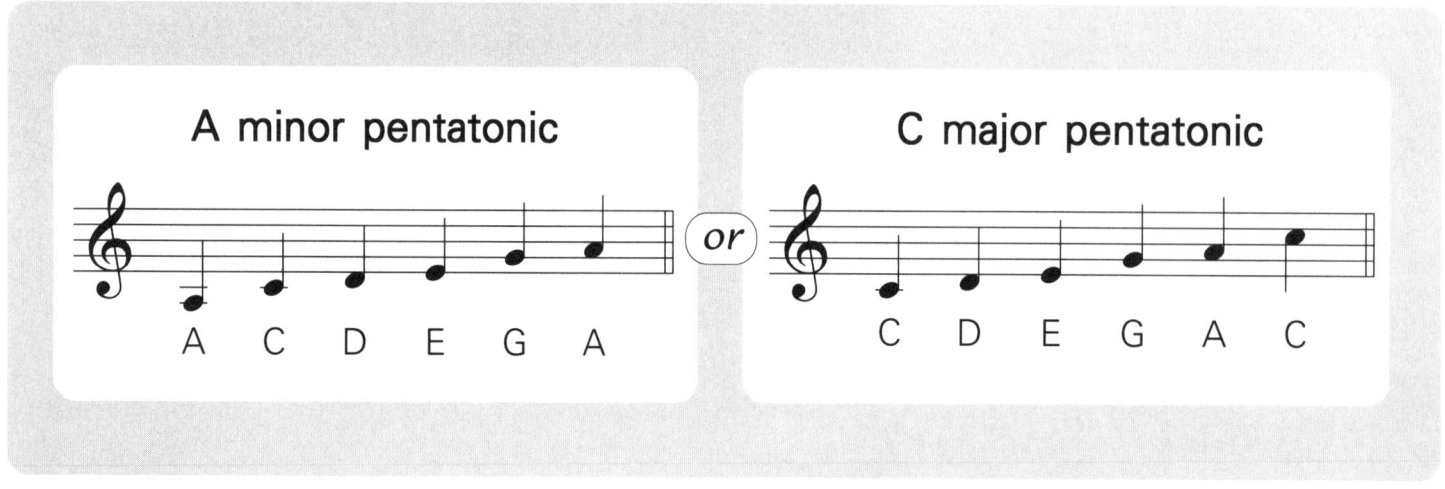

PENTATONIC THRILL #1

Tracks 5-8

*M*ake sure you are solid on everything up to this point before going any further.

PENCILQUIZ 2

1. On the opposite page are staves for you to do some more writing. I have left out the treble clef, so you can draw it in.

    Here's how I do it: | + ⌒ = 𝄞

    Now you try:

    When drawing the treble clef on the staff, make sure the bottom curve creates a circle around the second line (G). The treble clef was originally called the "G Clef".

2. I have also left out the time signature. Use either $\frac{4}{4}$ or $\frac{3}{4}$ time, you make the choice. Again, use only the notes and rests you know, spacing them logically. Put a whole rest in there somewhere, and use some ties, too.

> *If you like composing, now would be a good time to purchase a pad of music paper. I like eight or ten staves per page, just regular notebook size (8 1/2 x 11). Make sure to get single staff. One more thing—it's important to have a margin on both sides of the staff, rather than having the staff run right off the edge of the page. It looks much cleaner and more professional.*

Note Reference

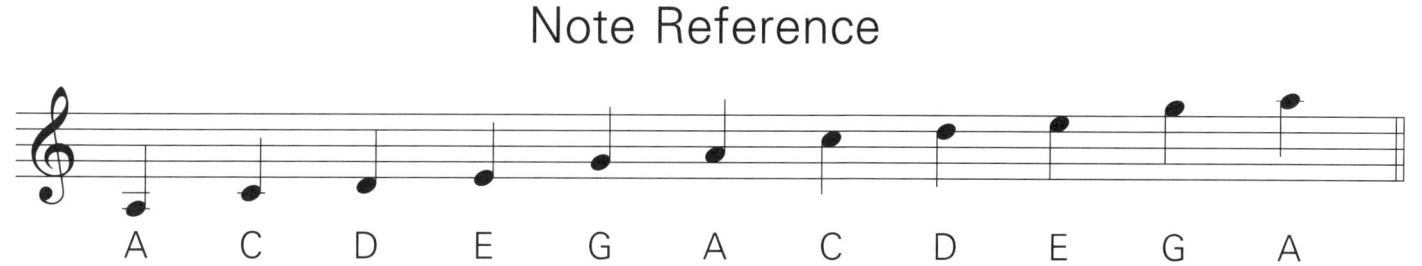

Lesson 7
Add *Lower* F

Adding **F** to the lower group completes the lower scale—from A to A.

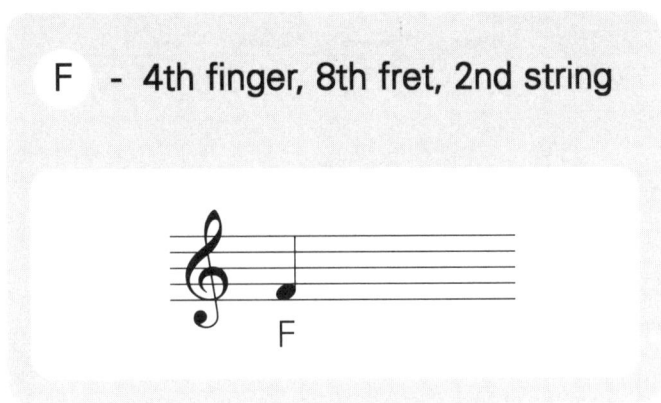

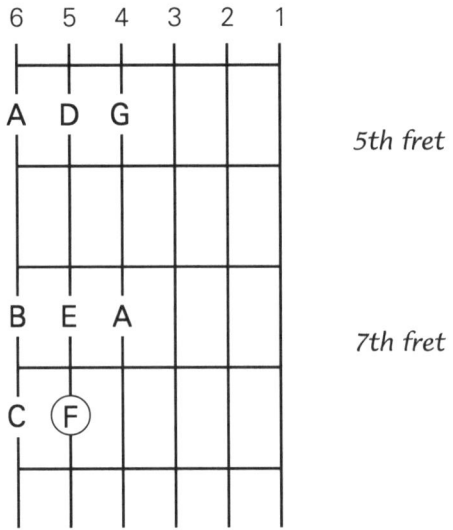

5th fret

7th fret

Eighth Notes

beamed eighth notes

unbeamed eighth notes

In $\frac{4}{4}$ time, an eighth note is worth half a beat (two eighth notes equal one beat). They are counted like this:

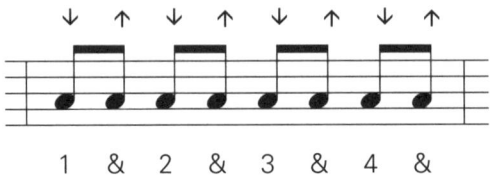

1 & 2 & 3 & 4 &

When learning to read eighth notes, it's best to pick all the "beats" with down strokes, and all the "ands" with up strokes (see arrows in example above).

Note Reference

A B C D E F G A G F E D C B

30

In the following examples, the pick follows a consistent pattern of down strokes and up strokes. This helps keep time with your hand. The second example is the same as the first, except that there happens to be a note to pick on the way up.

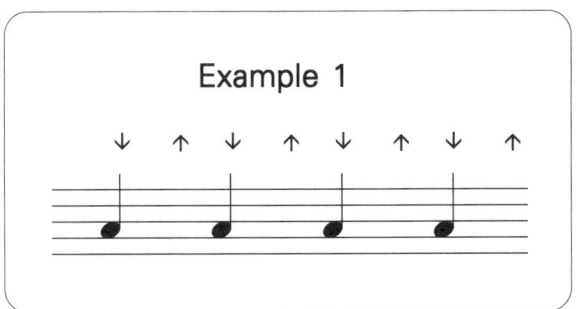
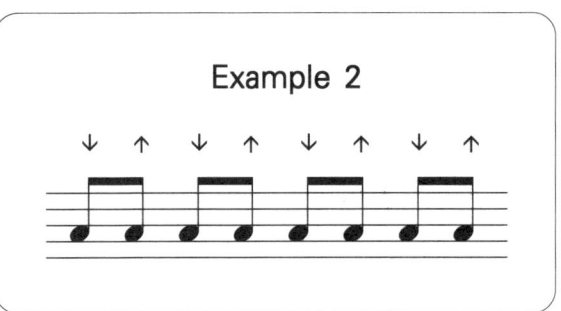

EXERCISE 7

Tracks 5-8

Lesson 8
Add *Higher* F

The addition of higher **F** gives us a complete major scale.

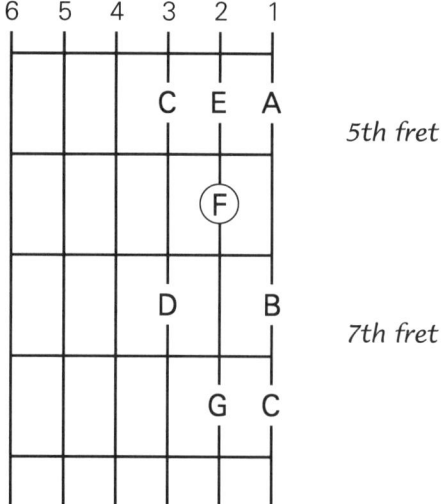

In Exercise 8, the third line can be very challenging. Make sure your picking includes the usual four down strokes and four up strokes. You will actually be making string contact on more up strokes than down strokes.

Note Reference

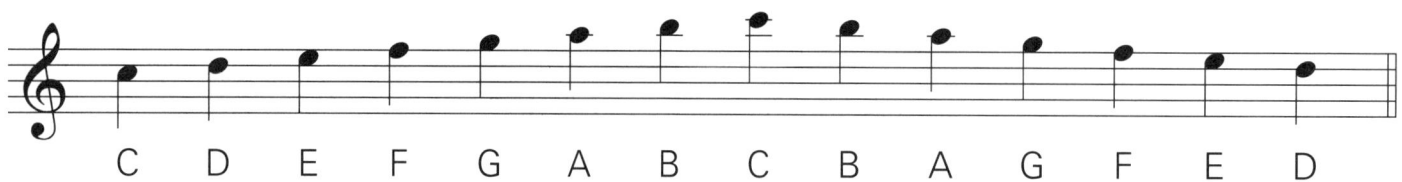

EXERCISE 8

Tracks 5-8

*P*ractice the new notes for a while, before proceeding.

SONG EXERCISE #4: *Rebel Without a Pause*

 A STACCATO mark is a small dot over or under a note. It means you don't let the note ring for its full value. As soon as you hear the note, stifle it, leaving some silence before the next note. For example, ♩ ♩ ♩ would sound like dah dah dah, where as ♩̇ ♩ ♩ sounds like <u>dut</u> dah dah. To stifle the ringing, ease up on your finger (left hand) immediately after playing the note.

On this tune you'll notice some whole rests. It will seem kind of strange, since, technically, a whole rest is worth four counts. But someone decided a whole rest could be used for a whole measure, even if the song is in another time signature, such as $\frac{3}{4}$. I've seen it, and now you've seen it. They will be worth three counts, in this case.

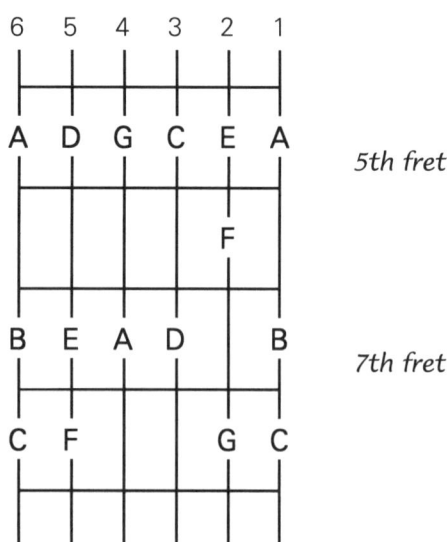

Note Reference

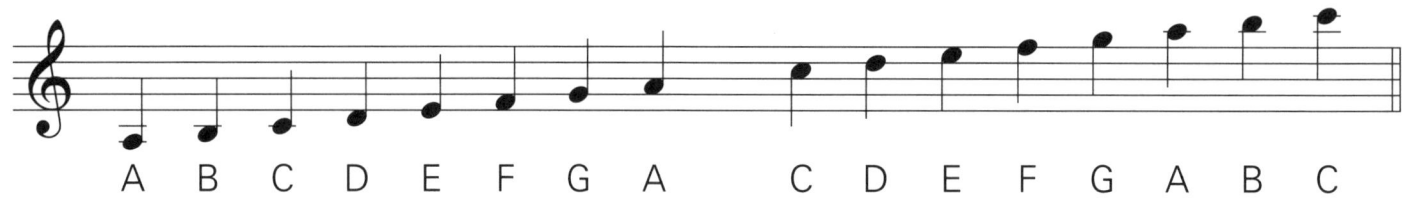

34

Rebel Without a Pause

Jerry Jennings

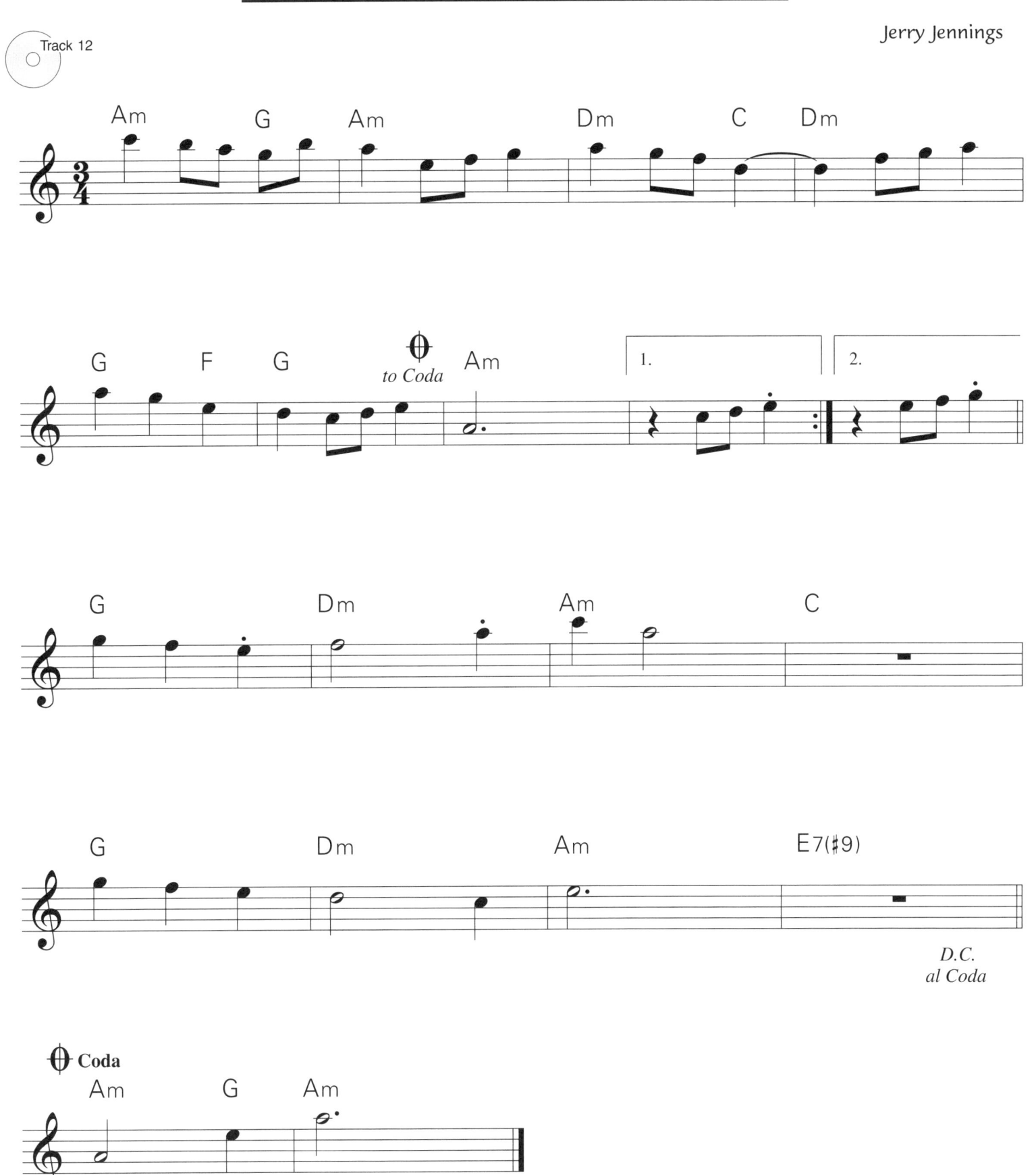

SONG EXERCISE #5: *Bar None*

Power Chords

On this tune, power chords are used throughout. They are indicated with a "5" because they contain a *root* and a *fifth*. No *third* is present, therefore major or minor is not an issue. (See Appendix 1 for bar chord information.)

Since this is kind of an 80s style rhythm, let's use a palm mute. Just rest the heel of your right hand on the bridge of the guitar in a way that some palm flesh touches the strings. You can regulate the amount of muting by how much palm is on the strings.

Use this rhythm, playing all down strokes:

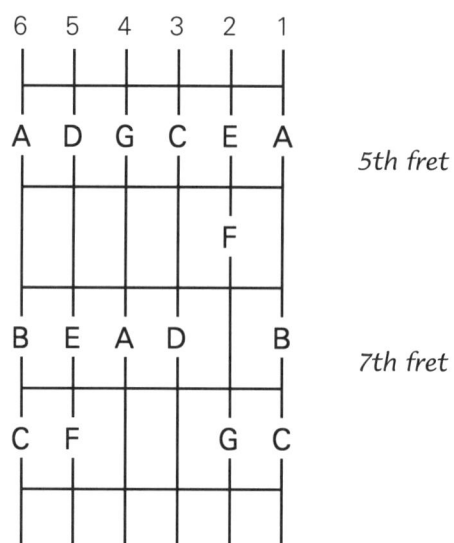

Note Reference

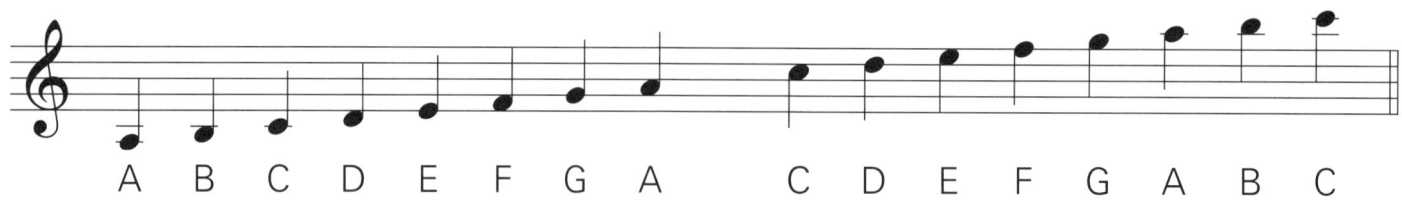

Bar None

Jerry Jennings

Lesson 9
Middle B

I saved middle *B* for last, because it's a little strange. This middle B is outside of our now familiar 5th position. You actually have to move your left hand into the *4th position* (first finger on fourth fret). While you are in the 4th position, it will be necessary to play the surrounding notes with different fingers than usual. No need to panic. Since we're focusing on the 5th position, we will only be taking short detours into the 4th position.

B - 1st finger, 4th fret, 3rd string

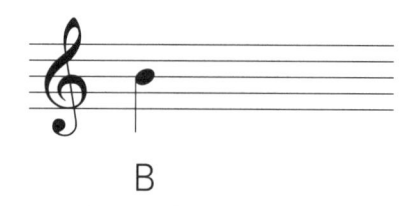

It's a good idea to practice playing up and down this pattern without looking, so your eyes can be free to read.

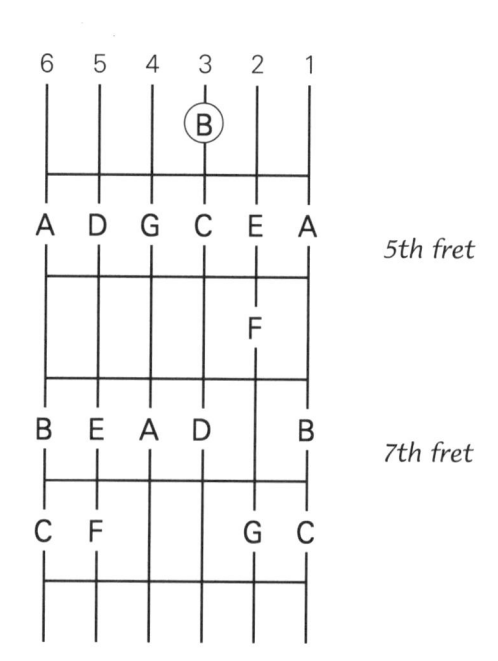

DOTTED QUARTER NOTE
(worth one and one-half beats)

Note Reference

A B C D E F G A B C D E F G A B C

GRACE NOTE

A GRACE NOTE looks like a miniature eighth note, seen with or without a slash through the stem (see bars nine, ten, and fifteen). The sound of the grace note is so short that it's not necessary to account for its time value (you hear just a hint of it prior to an actual note).

There are a few ways to approach a grace note. One way is with a *bend*. In bar nine, the grace note is a **G** and the actual note is an **A**. The **A** you usually play (1st string, 5th fret) is not played. Instead, play the **G** note with your fourth finger and bend the string immediately upward to the sound of the real note (**A**). Bending can be tough when using your fourth finger (as in bar nine) so it's O.K. to add your third finger for extra strength. Another way is with a *slide* (if bending is too hard, do the slide). In bar nine, you would start on the 8th fret of the 2nd string (**G**) and as you pick, begin sliding up to the 10th fret (**A**).

Since *one finger per fret in the 5th position* will no longer be a constant, I have placed numbers in the exercise below to indicate which finger to use. This is not uncommon in music intended for guitar.

Tracks 5-8

EXERCISE 9

Pentatonic Thrills #2

Here again, is the A minor pentatonic shape.

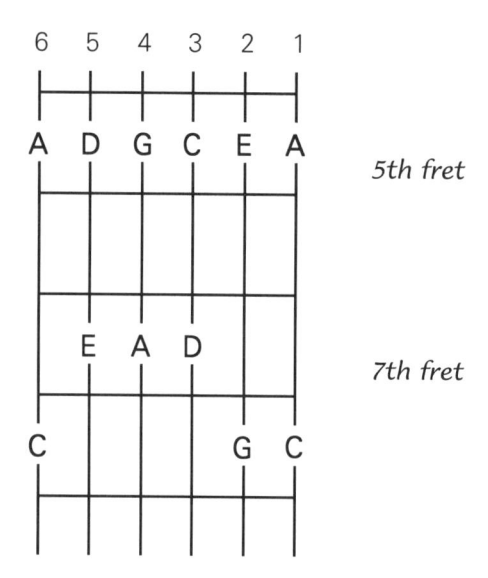

```
          6   5   4   3   2   1
          |   |   |   |   |   |
          A   D   G   C   E   A     5th fret
          
                      E   A   D     7th fret
          
          C                   G   C
```

Pull Offs
p/o

PULL OFFS are indicated by a slur (⌒) and the designation "p/o." They are placed between two notes on the staff. This sign means don't pick the string to play the second note, but pluck it with your left-hand finger. Example: In the first measure of line five, we have an E note, picked as usual. The following note (after the p/o sign) is a D. Now, make sure your first finger is already waiting on the D note while you're playing the E. Then, instead of just lifting your third finger off the string, pull it off with a downward motion. This will sound the D note without picking the string.

A minor pentatonic

A C D E G A C D E G A

Here are more A minor pentatonic thrills, this time using eighth notes. Make sure to accent where indicated (>).

Eighth notes can be in larger groups. In 4/4 time, it's common to group them as four eighth notes on beats 1 and 2 and on beats 3 and 4, but not for beats 2 and 3, since the middle of the measure needs to be a clear division point (for easier reading).

PENTATONIC THRILL #2

Tracks 5-8

Lesson 10
Flats (♭)

A FLAT symbol looks kind of like a lowercase *b* and *lowers* the note by one *half step* (one fret). It's placed in front of the note and lowers not only *it*, but all of the same note for the rest of that measure (unless canceled by a natural sign).

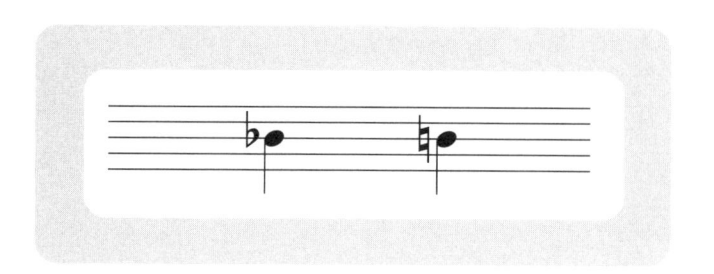

Example: In Exercise 10 on the first measure of line two, a **B** note is flatted on beat 2. When another **B** shows up on beat 4 (same measure), it's flat, too. The only way to make that second **B** not flat would be to place a NATURAL sign (♮) in front of it. That's what is happening in the first measure of line three.

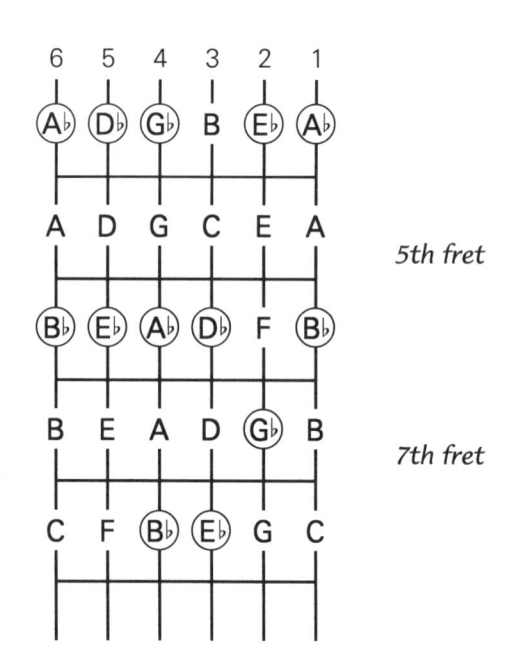

EIGHTH REST
(worth one-half beat of silence)

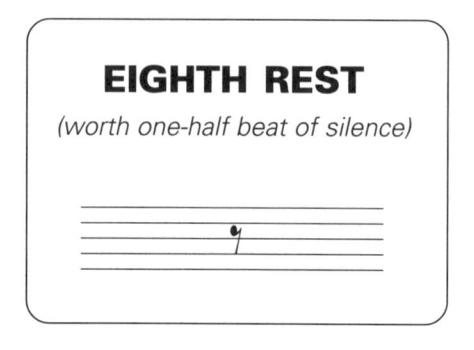

Note Reference

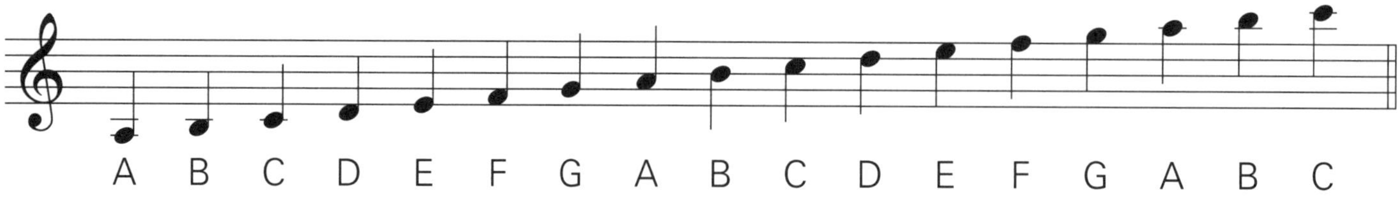

A B C D E F G A B C D E F G A B C

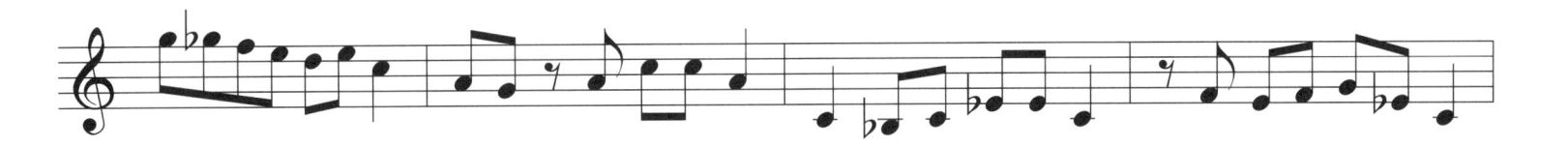

EXERCISE 10

Lesson 11
Sharps (♯)

A SHARP symbol looks kind of like a tick-tack-toe diagram and *raises* the note by one *half step* (one fret). The sharp is placed in front of the note. Again, all of the same note for the duration of that measure will be sharp, unless canceled by a natural sign.

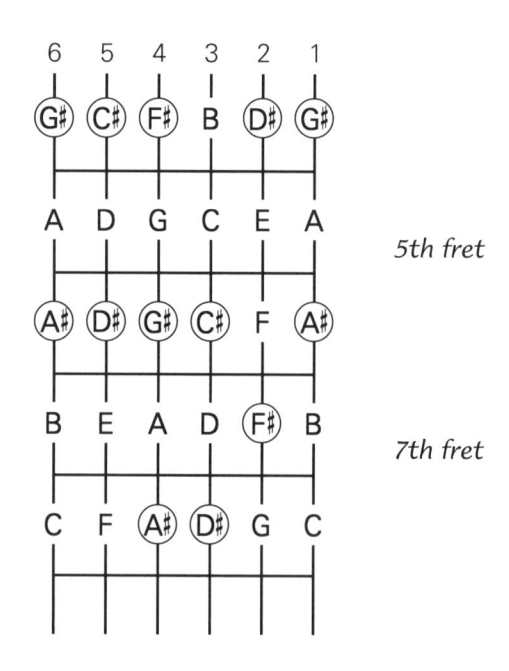

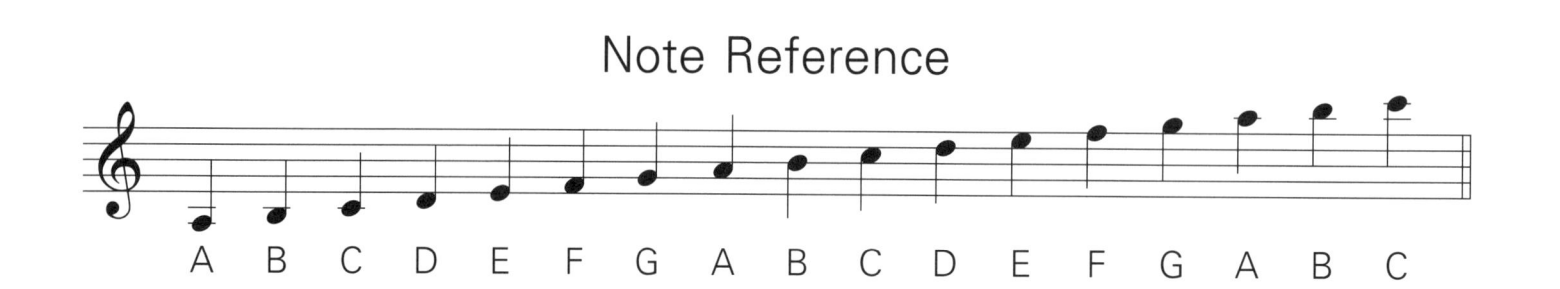

Note Reference

A B C D E F G A B C D E F G A B C

EXERCISE 11

Pentatonic Thrills #3

Now it will be possible to extract more pentatonic shapes! With the exception of E minor pentatonic, all of these can be done one-finger-per-fret in the 5th position.

C minor pentatonic

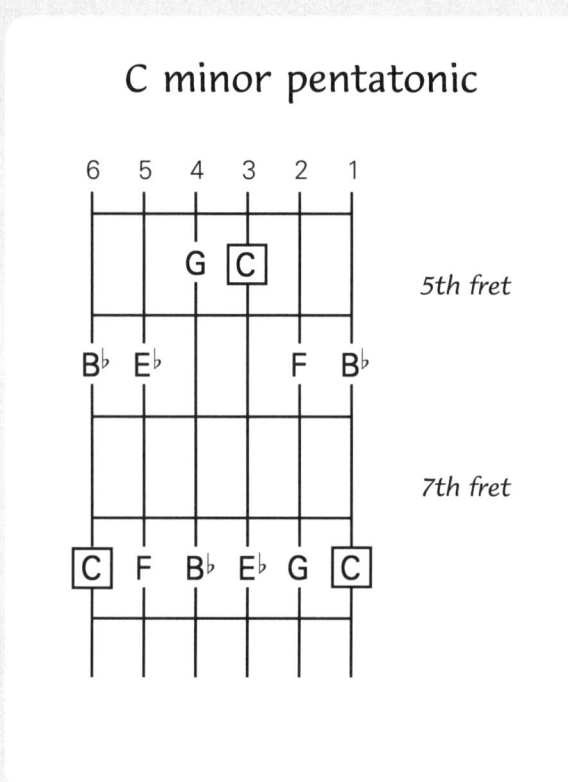

```
6   5   4   3   2   1
            G  [C]
                        5th fret
B♭  E♭         F   B♭

                        7th fret
[C] F   B♭ E♭  G  [C]
```

D minor pentatonic

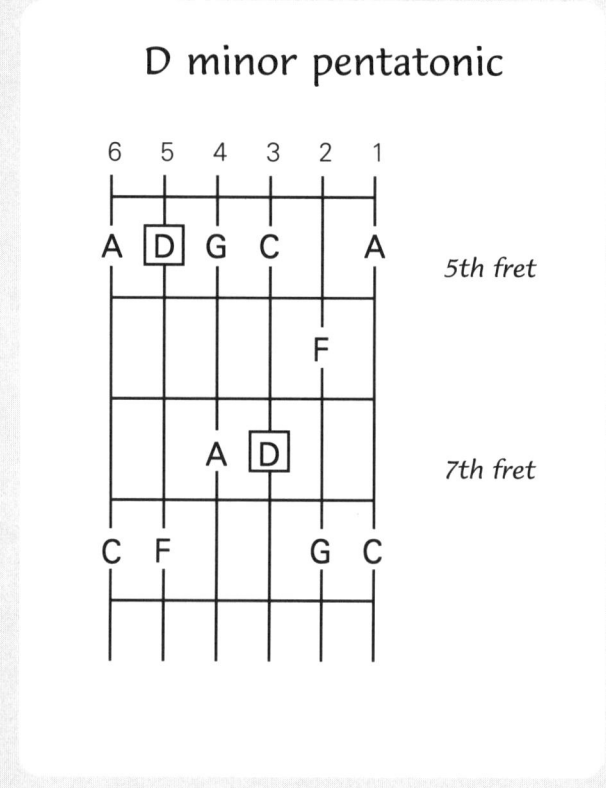

```
6   5   4   3   2   1
A  [D]  G   C       A
                        5th fret
                F
                        7th fret
        A  [D]
C   F           G   C
```

G minor pentatonic

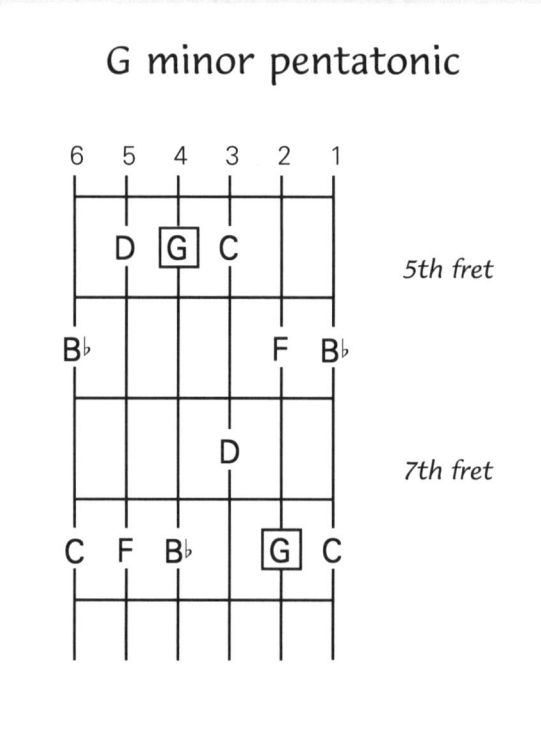

```
6   5   4   3   2   1
    D  [G]  C
                        5th fret
B♭             F   B♭

        D
                        7th fret
C   F   B♭ [G]  C
```

E minor pentatonic

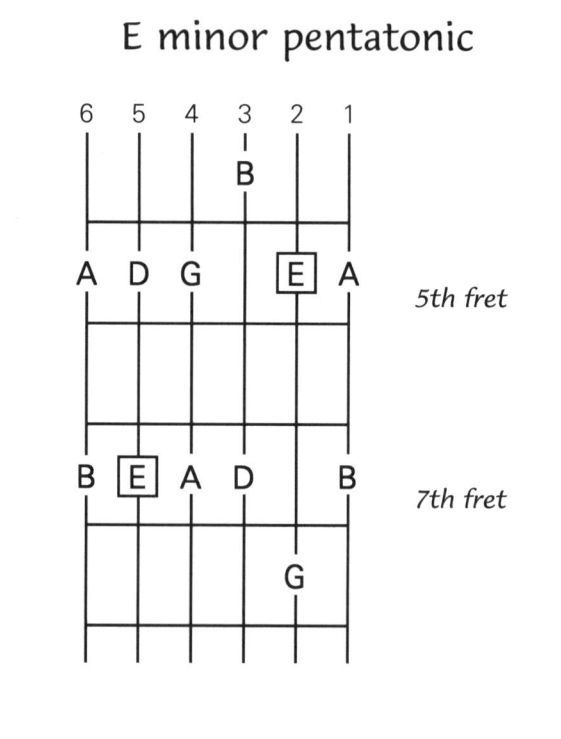

```
6   5   4   3   2   1
                B
A   D   G  [E]  A
                        5th fret

B  [E]  A   D       B
                        7th fret
                G
```

46

PENTATONIC THRILL #3

Tracks 5-8

C minor pentatonic

D minor pentatonic

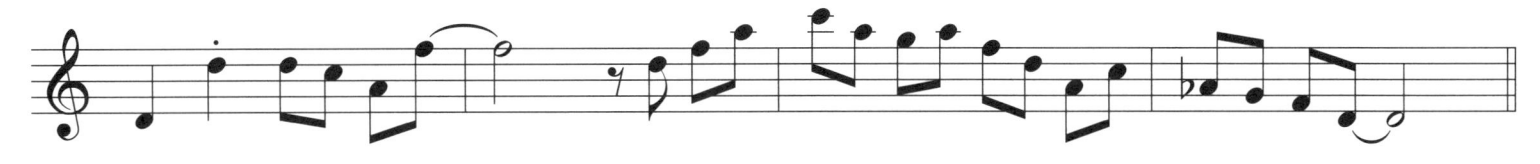

G minor pentatonic

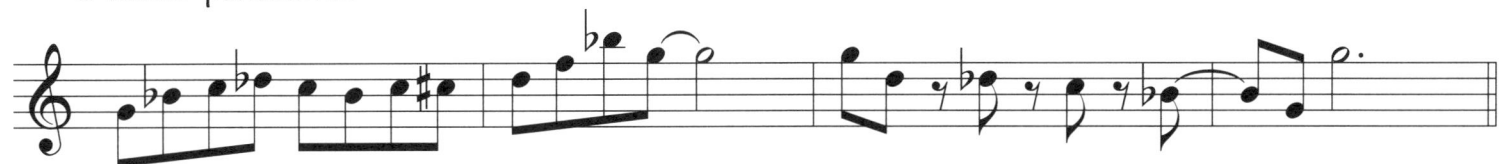

E minor pentatonic

Note Reference

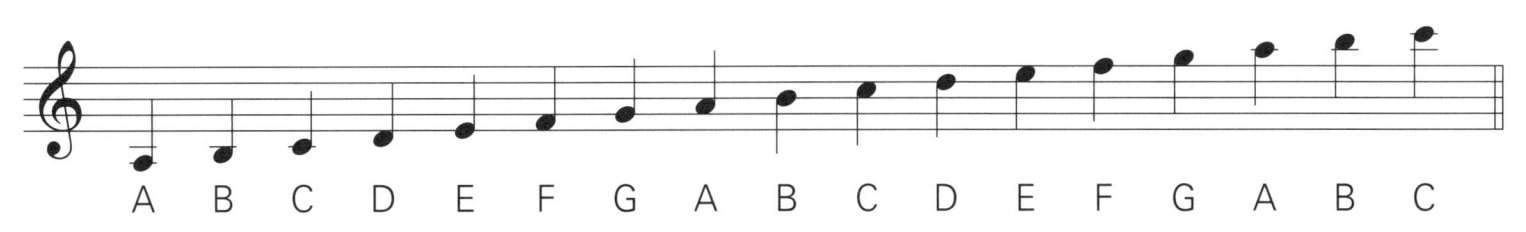

A B C D E F G A B C D E F G A B C

Lesson 12

New Time Signatures: 6/8 & 12/8

Up to now, we've worked with only two time signatures, 4/4 and 3/4. Because the bottom number is a four on both of these time signatures, we have been counting quarter notes. Example: In 3/4 time, we say "one, two, three," and in that time three quarter notes elapse (or six eighth notes, or a quarter note and four eighth notes, *etc.*).

Now with 6/8 time, an eight is on the bottom. This means we will be counting eighth notes instead of quarter notes. So when we say "one, two, three," only three eighth notes have elapsed. If the tempo is the same, we would now say it twice as fast because we are counting eighth notes.

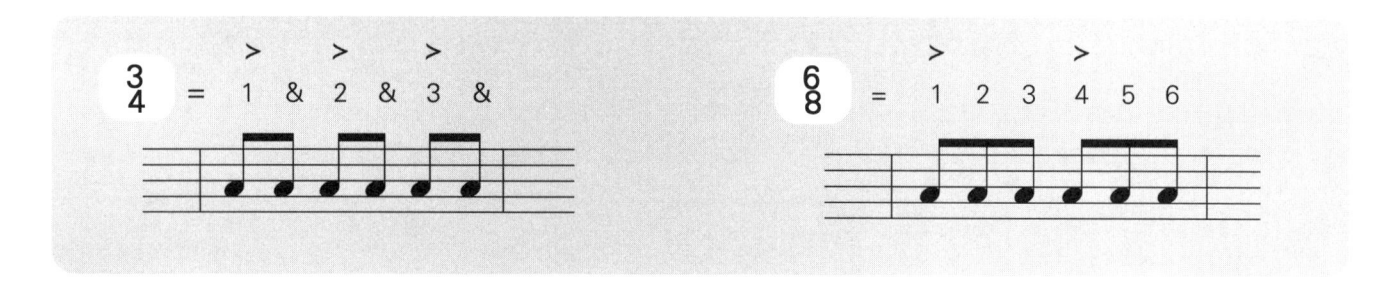

A measure of 3/4 and a measure of 6/8 each contain the same amount of time, but the feel is different. 3/4 is counted as three beats, whereas 6/8 is usually counted as two beats (each beat containing three eighth notes). Notice the accents in the diagram above.

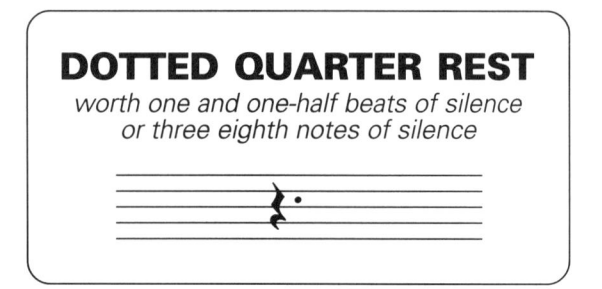

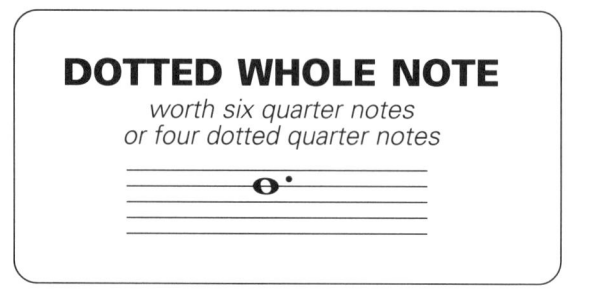

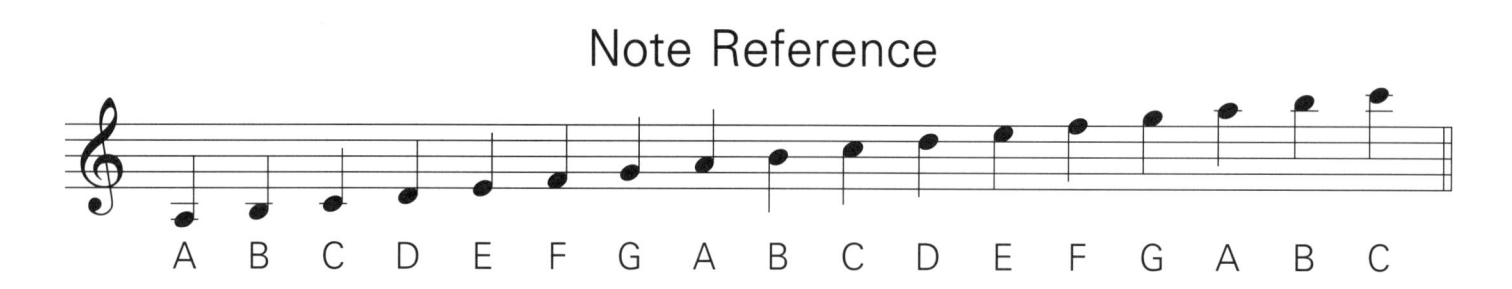

DOTTED QUARTER REST
worth one and one-half beats of silence or three eighth notes of silence

DOTTED WHOLE NOTE
worth six quarter notes or four dotted quarter notes

Note Reference

A B C D E F G A B C D E F G A B C

48

EXERCISE 12

12/8 Now instead of counting two sets of three, it's four sets of three. Just count to four, like in 4/4 except that each beat is a triplet.

SONG EXERCISE #6: *Funky Weather*

Key Signature

When all instances of a certain note are to be made sharp (or flat), a KEY SIGNATURE is used. In this tune, we will be in the key of one sharp. Whenever one sharp is in the key signature, that sharped note will be F#. This key signature is known as the "key of G." When you play from G to G (using an F#), you get a G major scale. Up until now, we've been using the key signature of C (no sharps or flats). When you go from C to C, you get a C major scale.

Key of G

ACCIDENTALS are sharps, flats, or naturals occurring during the tune, which deviate from the key signature. Until now, all sharps and flats we've used have been accidentals.

Traffic Signs

𝄋 **D.S.** (dal Segno) works just like D.C., but instead of going back to the beginning, you go back to the sign (𝄋).

𝄇 Repeat Loop—When you see a repeat sign, you go back to the beginning unless it is preceded by a backward repeat sign.

SLASH CHORDS

In this example, **FMaj7/A**, you play an FMaj7 chord over an A bass note. The slash is used when the bass note differs from the letter name of the chord.

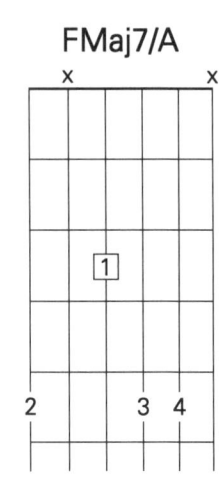

FMaj7/A
5th fret

Note Reference

A B C D E F G A B C D E F G A B C

Funky Weather

Jerry Jennings

SONG EXERCISE #7: *Some Kind of Blues*

Shuffle

There are two ways to interpret written music, shuffle (swing) or straight. In this example, each beat could be divided as we've always done it—directly in half.

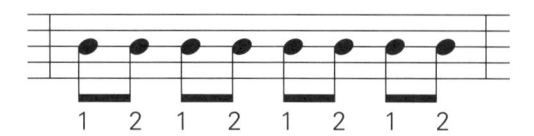

The other interpretation is more or less in thirds. A shuffle is often called "triplet feel." Each beat then is going to be divided like this:

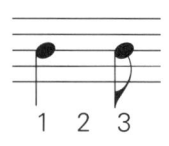

Notice that the first part of the beat is worth two eighth notes and the "and" is worth only one. Here's what the measure sounds like:

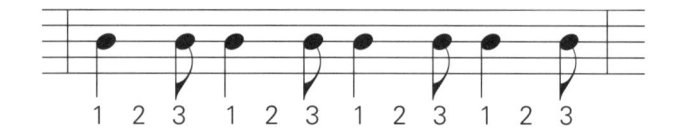

It's just like $\frac{12}{8}$! At the top of the page, on the left, it will say "shuffle," "swing," "triplet feel," or "$\frac{12}{8}$ feel." They all mean essentially the same thing. In fact, very seldom do I actually write in $\frac{12}{8}$. I usually use $\frac{4}{4}$ and then just write "shuffle" at the top. When three equal notes do occur in the beat, they are indicated as a triplet so you don't mistake them for three eighth notes equaling one and one-half beats. (See bar 23)

Pick Up Notes

Notice the first three notes of this tune are not enough to equal four beats (one measure). These notes are called PICK UP notes, or just *the pick up*. Bar one starts after the pick up. Since all <u>complete</u> measures begin with "one," these pick up notes would be counted as "and four and" (the tail end of a measure).

More on Keys

The key of no sharps or flats is the key of C, technically. But sometimes it is easier to start with a blank slate and add accidentals even though a tune is not in C, *per se*.

> *NC* means no chord. The rhythm player stops playing.

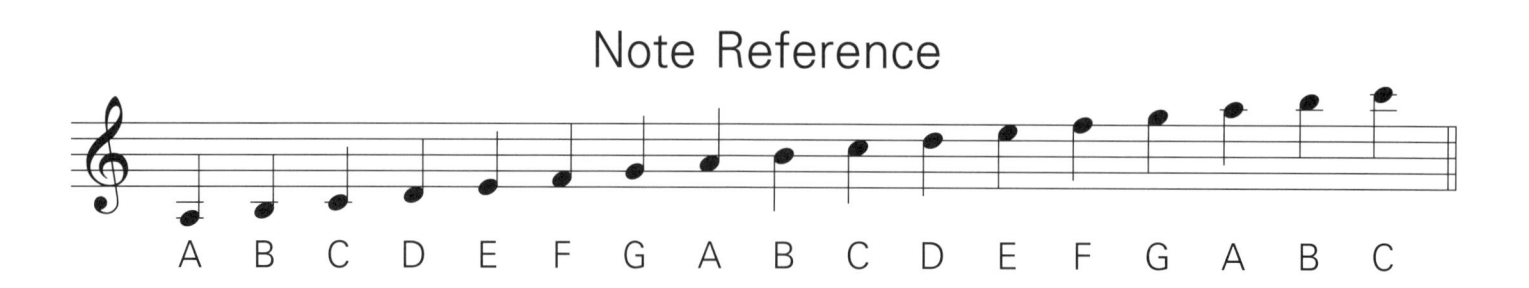

Note Reference

A B C D E F G A B C D E F G A B C

Some Kinda Blues

Jerry Jennings

Medium shuffle

SONG EXERCISE #8: *Bossa de Hot Sauce*

Another Key Signature

One flat in the key signature means you are in the key of F. Whenever you have one flat in the key signature, that flatted note will be B♭. Again, it is the key of F because when you play from *F* to *F* using all natural notes, except *B* (which is flat), you get an F major scale.

Key of F

Traffic Sign

al Fine (after D.S. or D.C.) means the end. So instead of hitting a coda sign and skipping down to the next coda sign and continuing, you just end the song at the word "Fine."

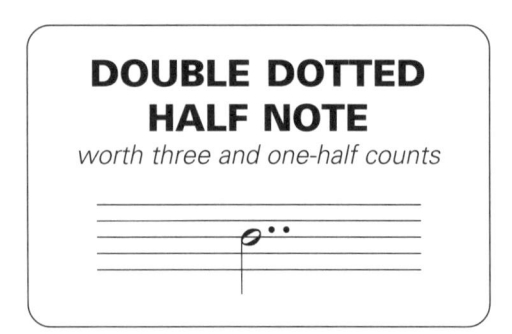

DOUBLE DOTTED HALF NOTE
worth three and one-half counts

Note Reference

A B C D E F G A B C D E F G A B C

54

Bossa de Hot Sauce

Jerry Jennings

CD Contents

Track 1	Lesson 1 - Note Time Values Explained
Track 2	Lesson 1 - Note Time Values Applied
Track 3	Lesson 1 - Four Bar Rhythmic Exercise
Track 4	Lesson 1 - Note Exercise / Pitches
Track 5	Metronome Track 70 bpm
Track 6	Metronome Track 90 bpm
Track 7	Metronome Track 110 bpm
Track 8	Metronome Track 130 bpm
Track 9	Song 1 - Avocados (minus melody)
Track 10	Song 2 - Traces of Thought (minus melody)
Track 11	Song 3 - Mirrors on Pluto (minus melody)
Track 12	Song 4 - Rebel Without a Pause (minus melody)
Track 13	Song 5 - Bar None (minus melody)
Track 14	Song 6 - Funky Weather (minus melody)
Track 15	Song 7 - Some Kinda Blues (minus melody)
Track 16	Song 8 - Bossa de Hot Sauce (minus melody)
Track 17	Song 1 - Avocados (melody version)
Track 18	Song 2 - Traces of Thought (melody version)
Track 19	Song 3 - Mirrors on Pluto (melody version)
Track 20	Song 4 - Rebel Without a Pause (melody version)
Track 21	Song 5 - Bar None (melody version)
Track 22	Song 6 - Funky Weather (melody version)
Track 23	Song 7 - Some Kinda Blues (melody version)
Track 24	Song 8 - Bossa de Hot Sauce (melody version)
Track 25	Tuning Track

APPENDIX #1

Chord Families

Major	Usually no indication is necessary, just the letter name. Example: C, E♭, D, F♯, *etc.*
Minor	Letter name followed by: m, mi, or – Example: A–, Dm, Emi, *etc.*
Dominant 7	Letter name followed by: 7 Example: E7, A7, F♯7, *etc.* (♯ applies to letter name, unless grouped otherwise in parentheses)
Major 7	Letter name followed by: Maj, Maj7, △, M7 Example: B♭△7, CMaj, GMaj7, DM7, *etc.*
Minor 7	Letter name followed by: m7, mi7, –7
Half Diminished	Letter name followed by: ⌀, ⌀7, m7(♭5)
Diminished	Letter name followed by: °, °7, dim
Augmented	Letter name followed by: Aug, +
Slash Chords	Chord "over" bass note (G/A). When the bass note differs from the letter name of the chord.

Chords

Since the objective of this book is sight reading, we don't have the space to do an in-depth study of moveable chords. The following pages contain a few essential chords, divided into two categories:

Type 1 The root is on the *sixth* string.
Type 2 The root is on the *fifth* string.

Just move the chord shape up or down the neck, until the root (□) is on the chord name you want.

57

Type 1

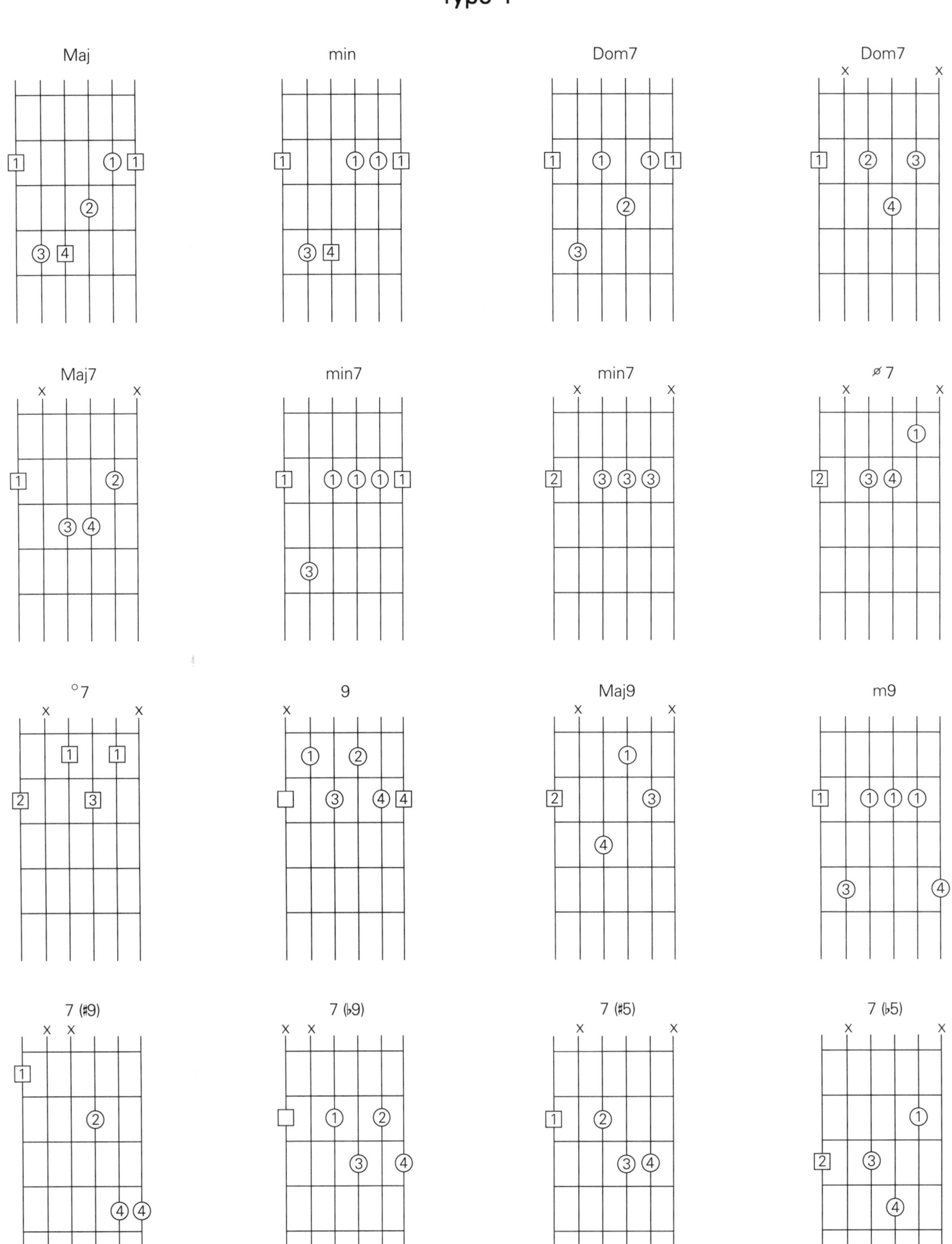

Type 2

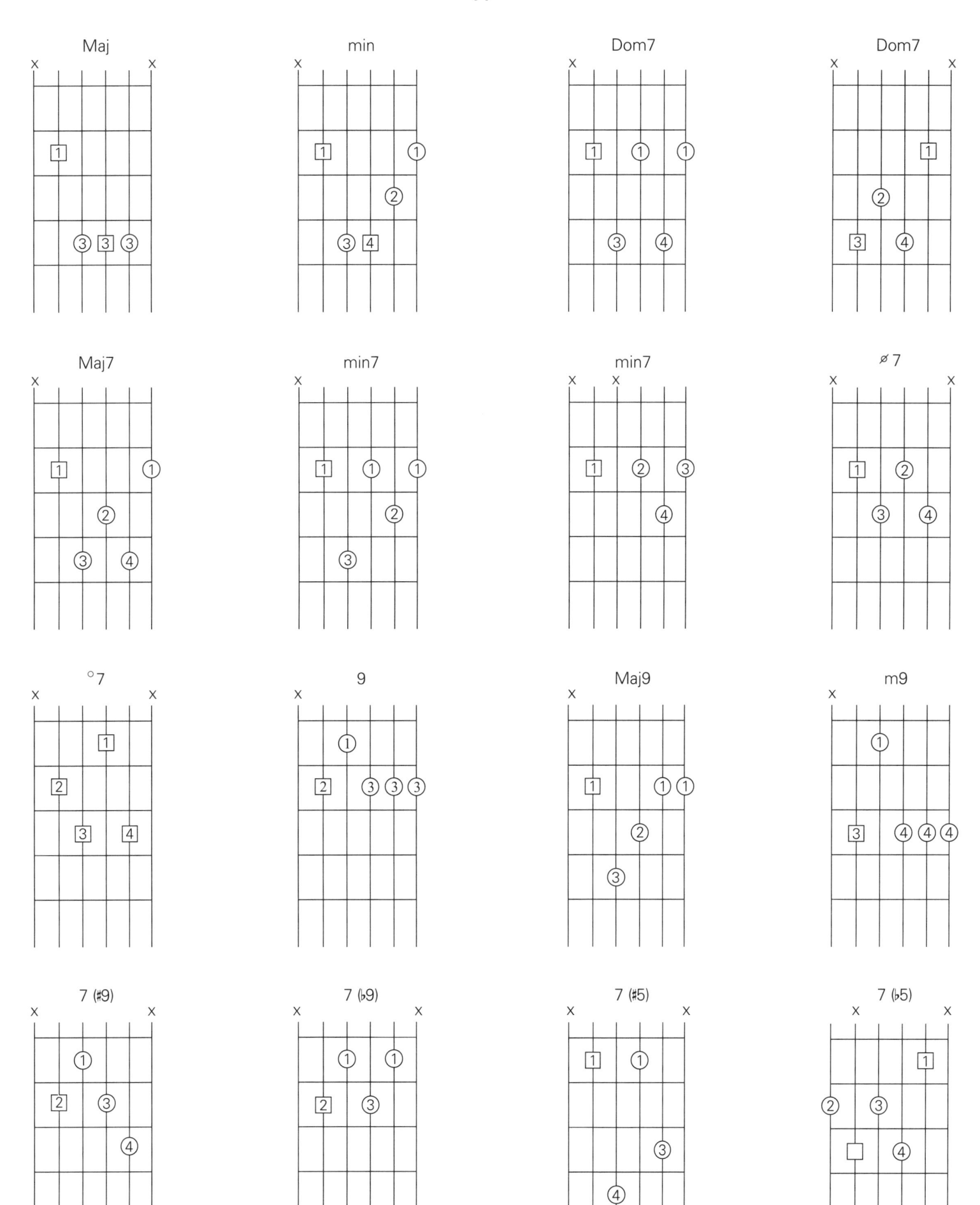

Power Chords

Power chords are indicated with a "5" because they contain a root and a fifth. No third is present, therefore major or minor is not an issue. Power chords are also moveable. Wherever you slide them, they get a new name based on the root (R).

TYPE 1

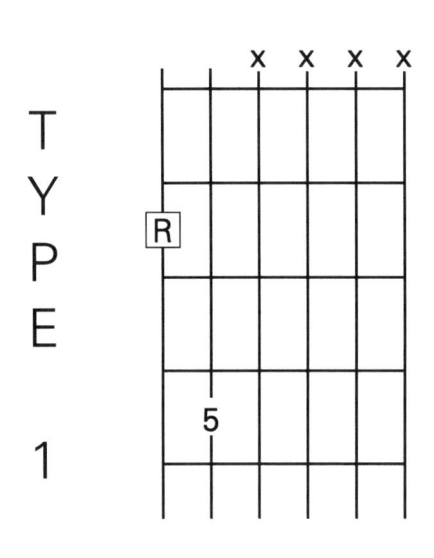

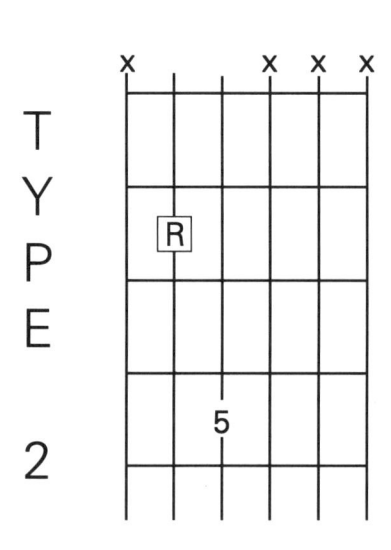

TYPE 2

All **type 1** chords have a root on the sixth string. All **type 2** chords have a root on the fifth string.

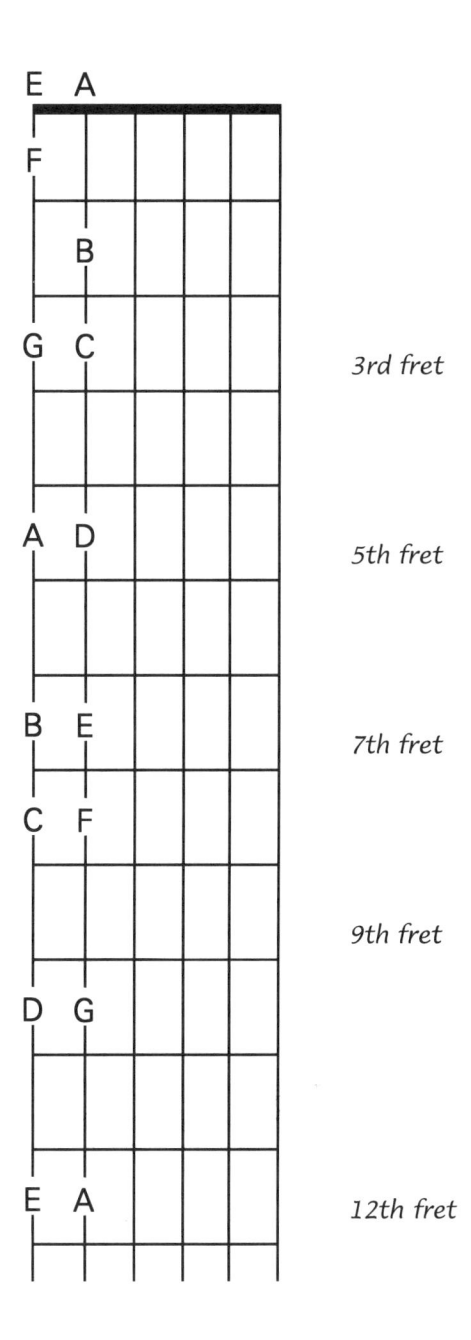

```
E  A
|  |
F  |
|  |
|  B
|  |
G  C                3rd fret
|  |
|  |
|  |
A  D                5th fret
|  |
|  |
|  |
B  E                7th fret
|  |
C  F
|  |
|  |                9th fret
|  |
D  G
|  |
|  |
|  |
E  A                12th fret
```

APPENDIX #2

Key Signatures

C Major—No Sharps or Flats

Key of:	Number of Sharps		Key of:	Number of Flats	
G	1	F	F	1	B
D	2	F, C	B♭	2	B, E
A	3	F, C, G	E♭	3	B, E, A
E	4	F, C, G, D	A♭	4	B, E, A, D
B	5	F, C, G, D, A	D♭	5	B, E, A, D, G
F♯	6	F, C, G, D, A, E	G♭	6	B, E, A, D, G, C
C♯	7	F, C, G, D, A, E, B	C♭	7	B, E, A, D, G, C, F

Order of Sharps—F C G D A E B
Fred Can Go Down An Elevator Backward

Order of Flats—B E A D G C F
Opposite of Sharps

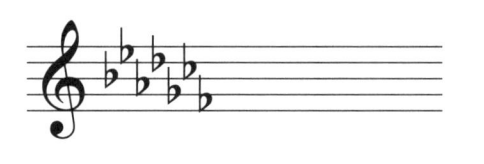

Circle of 5ths

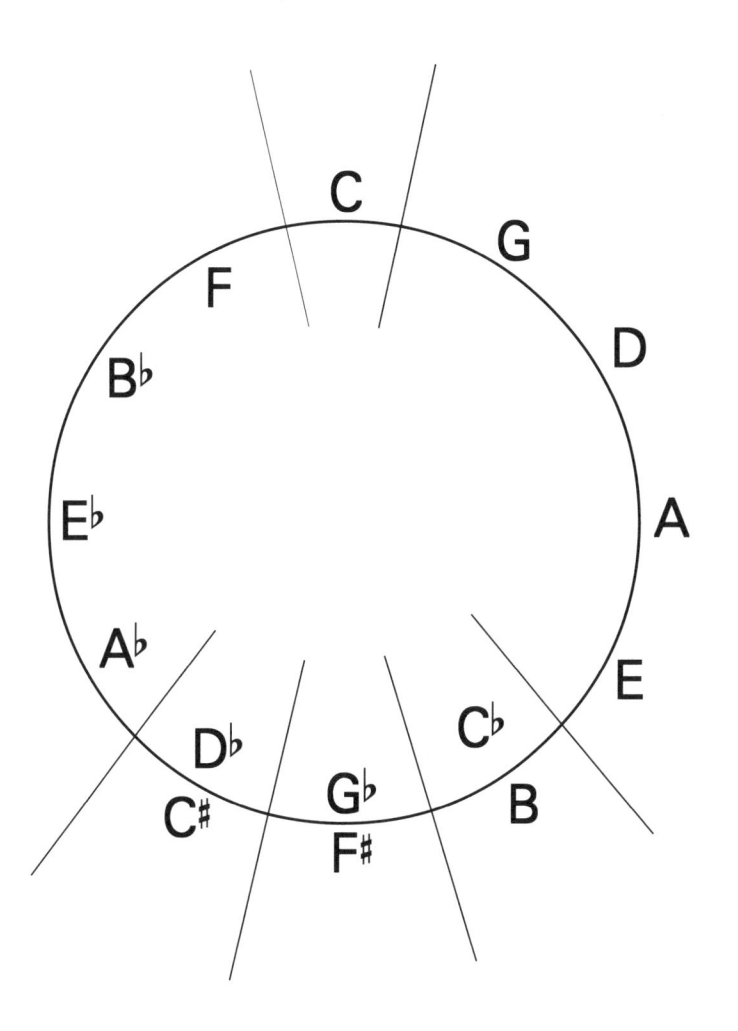

These are the twelve keys starting from C. As you move clockwise you add a sharp each time. (You are moving in fifths starting from C). And moving counterclockwise from C, you are adding a flat each time (moving in fourths). Some of the keys have two names. For example, D♭ and C♯ are the same set of notes. These are called *enharmonic equivalents*.

Thanks

I hope you've enjoyed the book and CD. Please visit our website at *www.jenningspub.com* for advanced exercises and new concepts. You may also want to purchase *The New Real Book* by Chuck Sher, which is a collection of jazz standards, available at most music stores. You'll find many tunes at your level, and some beyond. Find as many chances to read as you can, so you can keep growing in this area. If you are working with other players who do some reading, write stuff for each other. If you want to write parts for your bass player, you'll want to learn the bass clef. Check out *The Bassist's Link to Sight Reading*.

Thanks again,
JERRY JENNINGS